BEGINNER'S MIND

an introduction to
Zen Buddhism

Also by Tim Langdell from
StillCenter Publications:

*Christ Way, Buddha Way: Jesus as Wisdom
Teacher and a Zen Perspective on His Teachings*

Kenosis: Christian Self-Emptying Meditation

*The Practice of the Presence of God by Brother
Lawrence with a Christian Meditation
Practice Guide by Tim Langdell*

A series of books by Evelyn Underhill with Tim
Langdell (*Mysticism, Practical Mysticism, The
Mystic Way, The Essentials of Mysticism*)

Coming soon by Tim Langdell
from StillCenter Publications:

Now Voyager: The Art of Conscious Living

*Mindful Moment: Using Mindfulness to
Find Peace in a Stressful World*

By Tim Langdell
from Oxbridge Publishing

*The Rise of the Angeliti:
Book One of the Oxbridge Trilogy*

And with Cheri Langdell
from Praeger

*Coping with Vision Loss: Understanding the
Psychological, Social, and Spiritual Effects*

BEGINNER'S MIND

an introduction to
Zen Buddhism

TIM LANGDELL

StillCenter Publications
Oxbridge Publishing Inc
Pasadena, CA / Oxford, UK

StillCenter Publications
An imprint of Oxbridge Publishing Inc.
Oxford/Pasadena
530 South Lake Avenue, 171
Pasadena, CA 91101
www.oxbridgepublishing.com

Library of Congress Cataloging-in-Publication Data
Langdell, Tim
      Beginner's Mind: An Introduction to Zen Buddhism / Tim
Langdell
         pages cm
     ISBN: 0-9990928-2-0 (pbk)
     ISBN-13: 978-0-9990928-2-8 (pbk)
     1. Zen   2. Buddhism   3. Zen Buddhism   I. Title

Library of Congress Control Number: 2020944195

9 8 7 6 5 4 3 2 1

FIRST EDITION

"In the beginner's mind there
are many possibilities,
but in the expert's there are few."

Shunryu Suzuki

Dedicated to Wonji Dharma
(Paul Lynch)

Contents

preface

This book arose from a discussion in a Zen Teacher's group I am a member of where the consensus of the group was there is no single introduction to Zen that we could all whole-heartedly recommend. Of the many introductory works, there was agreement that some were too focused on one perspective of Zen, others too narrowly focused on another. Still others were worthy texts, but not very accessible for a beginner. And still others had much to commend them but were never intended as a truly inclusive introduction to Zen Buddhism. Thus, this book was born.

A challenge in writing a work like this is that there is a lot of misinformation about what Zen is. Indeed, even the word "Zen" has entered common usage to mean almost anything relating to being calm or minimalist. Worse, the word Zen being Japanese has given the false impression that Zen *is* Japanese: it is not, or at least not only Japanese. Zen originated in China where it was known as "*Chan*," being the Chinese transliteration of the Sanskrit word "*Dhyana*" meaning meditation.

So dominant has been the Japanese influence over the popularization of Zen in the West, that many now mistakenly believe Zen originated in Japan. The two best known branches of Zen—"Soto" and "Rinzai"—are also often mistakenly thought of as Japanese inventions. They are not.

This book then is a comprehensive summary of what Zen is, what its origins are, how it is practiced here in the West, and how you can practice it yourself.

T here is
    nothing
      either good
or bad, but thinking
makes it so.

William Shakespeare

one

What is Zen?

The word Zen has so extensively infused Western culture that that Merriam-Webster partly defines it as anything "having or showing qualities [of] calmness and acceptance." It is used as a brand name for anxiety relief pills, bubble bath, health spas and face cream. Zen has become associated with design simplicity ("that's very Zen"), minimalist architecture and spartan interior décor. For some, Zen is associated with archery, flower arrangement, poetry (haiku) or even—thanks to writer Robert Pirsig—motorcycle maintenance.

But Zen is none of this (yet in another sense, it is all of it—more on that later). Zen is a branch of Buddhism, specifically Mahayana Buddhism that came into being just over two thousand years ago around the same time as Christianity. The Mahayana school is also known as the "Greater Vehicle." The other main branch of Buddhism is the Theravada tradition ("The School of Elders") which is sometimes referred to as the Hinayana School ("Lesser Vehicle"). However, this is generally agreed to be a derogatory term coined by the newer Mahayana School.

Zen itself arose in China (as *Chan* Buddhism) around the 6th century C.E. when a Buddhist monk known as Bodhidharma brought it there. Why Zen is so attractive to many is because while Buddhism is a major world religion, here in the West, Zen is seen as a "way," a practice, or simply a spiritual path. Associated mainly with meditation, since it is non-theistic it is common for people to combine their Zen practice with their Jewish faith, Christianity, Islamic faith, and so on. Practicing Zen does not require giving up any other faith tradition or spiritual path. It also does not require that you "believe" in anything or become a formal member.

The word Zen is Japanese for the original Indian Sanskrit word *dhyana*, meaning meditation. But Zen is Chinese in origin, not Japanese, and is known in China as *Chan* Buddhism. "Chan" of course being a transliteration in Chinese of the Sanskrit word. The very fact we use the word Zen together with the heavy Japanese influence on Zen in the West, leads many to falsely believe that as a branch of Buddhism Zen is purely Japanese. This misunderstanding is added to by the proliferation of books written on Zen from a Japanese perspective, and particularly those based on Japanese Soto Zen, the main version of Zen practiced in the West.

From its roots in China, Zen first spread to Korea and Vietnam, then eventually spread to Japan before being introduced to the West. And here in the West, while Japanese Zen dominates, there are many centers and groups practicing Korean and Vietnamese Zen, too. In Korea it's called *Seon* and in Vietnam it's called *Thien*.

Zen is a Buddhist practice that focuses on gaining insight into one's true nature, with an emphasis on benefiting others. At its core, for most people it is a simply a meditation practice, sitting what is widely known by its Japanese term "zazen" (literally, "seated meditation"). But it would be a mistake to think of Zen as merely a meditation practice aimed at helping you to de-stress and feel calmer. While Zen often has those benefits, it is far more than just a calming meditation exercise.

What is Zen in the West?

In the West, the practice of Zen varies widely from center to center, group to group. Not only are there significant differences between the practices of Chinese, Korean, Vietnamese and Japanese Zen, even within a branch of Zen practices can vary significantly from one Zen center to another. Zen runs the gamut from small "sitting" groups that meet weekly simply to sit zazen, through to established Zen centers that have an abbot, Zen priests and monks living on the premises, and which hold retreats, have liturgy services, as well as regular zazen and one-on-one sessions with a Zen teacher (called *dokusan*, Jp).

Within the Japanese tradition, for instance, there are two well-known schools of Zen: Soto and Rinzai. Again, while many mistakenly believe these two schools originated in Japan, they didn't. Soto was founded in China as the *Caodong School* and Rinzai is the Japanese line of the Chinese *Linji School* ("Rinzai" being the Japanese pronunciation of the Chinese characters 临 济 for "Linji"). The most common form of Zen in the West is Japanese Soto Zen, which has a focus on meditation ("zazen"). The other school, Rinzai, focuses more on koan introspection.

Central to Zen is becoming aware of your true nature, or "waking up." "Buddha" simply means "the awakened one." We'll talk about what this "waking up" means later in this book, but two main routes to this waking in Zen are meditation and koan introspection. Because fewer Zen centers in the West use koans than those that practice pure zazen, people tend to be less familiar with the term koan. If you've heard of koans, then you likely have heard of the misquoted one, "What is the sound of one hand clapping?" In fact, coincidently, as I was writing this

5

the question on the television quiz show *Jeopardy* was asking contestants, "*Which religion is associated with the sound of one hand clapping?*"

However, that is not the actual koan, but a corrupted version of it that has entered popular culture. The actual koan asks: "*Two hands clap and there is a sound. What is the sound of the single hand?*" This koan, and a humorous "solution" to it, has even appeared on the TV Show "The Simpsons." To the uninitiated, koans appear to be pithy riddles to solve. But they are not. Rather, koans and zazen have the same purpose—to help one fully awaken to the present moment, and to realize one's true self.

What to Expect When You Start Practicing

But you won't find koans taught at most smaller sitting groups. Rather, what you will experience is a small group of people who meet to sit for about 20-30 minutes, perhaps as long as 40 minutes. For many groups there may then be a brief period of walking meditation (Japanese: *kinhin*), followed by a second session of zazen. Occasionally, these sitting sessions may be preceded or followed by some kind of "social" time. Less frequently, where the meeting is being run by a Zen teacher, there may be a so-called *dharma talk* (Japanese: *teisho*—although some may reserve this term for a more formal talk by a Zen master or senior teacher).

Don't be surprised if the small sitting group you find meets in almost complete silence. When arriving members may greet each other in muted tones, leaving their shoes at the door as is customary. Each attendee may then simply go to their cushion or chair and prepare for meditation in silence. Either by striking a bell or a singing bowl, the meditation starts, ending with a further strike of the bell or bowl. If there is to be walking meditation, then you will find members know what to do and simply start walking. Any talking will likely be frowned on, thus new attendees need to be trained on what to expect and what to do before the formal "sitting" session commences.

Hence, attendees arrive and having removed their shoes proceed to where they will sit and make a slight bow toward the chair or cushion while holding their hands at chest height in what is called "gassho"—this resembles hands in prayer:

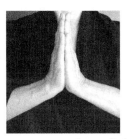

Then each person turns to make a slight bow, hands still in gassho, toward the others in the group. Then each will sit and place their hands in what is known as the cosmic mudra:

The attendees wait patiently while others arrive in as close to silence as they can, and when all are ready the bell or bowl is struck. If when the bell next sounds there is to be walking meditation, each attendee will know to stand, turn to straighten their cushion, turn again towards the others, and bow in gassho. Then the person running the session may use a bell or wooden clappers to indicate the walking commences. Attendees then turn to the left a quarter turn, and start walking with head bowed slightly, taking a small step with every in breath.

Of course, as you will find is usual in Zen, each practice group will probably do things differently—sometimes the differences can be minor (which can be very confusing), sometimes a group will do things in a totally different way from the last group you attended. For instance, some groups may not do walking meditation, and some who do it will have second clapper or bell sound to indicate that the walking should speed up for the second half of the walking period. While it's a very broad generalization, Soto Zen groups tend to favor the slow walking, whereas Rinzai groups walk faster.

In their minimal format, such sitting groups are just an opportunity for attendees to do almost exactly what they do at home, but in a group setting. Few words are spoken, there is just one or two sessions of zazen, and then attendees bow to each other before leaving in silence. Little social interaction happens, no chit chat, no dharma talk, no discussion. But this is "Zen lite," for a more complete immersion in Zen you would need to visit a Zen center, or a smaller group run by a trained teacher.

While it is an over-generalization, Zen centers based on Korean Zen tradition tend to be less formal than those with roots in Japanese tradition. Some have said that this is in part because in Japan Zen became influenced by the *Bushido* tradition of the *samurai* warriors. Of course, since *Bushido* emerged some centuries after Zen first flowered in Japan, the influence is likely from Zen to *Bushido*. But the underlying militaristic precision of behavior and ceremony suffuses

Japanese culture, showing itself in the tea ceremony and in other ways.

Attending a Japanese style Zen center will thus likely involve learning a number of rules that must be followed. I recall when I first attended Zen Center of Los Angeles, I felt like I just couldn't do anything right. I was wearing fairly colorful "hippie" clothing (in my defense, it was the very early 1970s). This was clearly frowned upon: I would need to acquire at the very least black yoga pants and a black t shirt, better still I should invest in a more formal black samu jacket (or *samue, samugi*—samu means daily work and it's a jacket that traditionally worn by monks to do their daily chores, and which crosses over at the front and ties in place on one side).

My wardrobe issues resolved, I then noticed widespread bowing in gassho (palms together in front of the chest). To me, as one uninitiated, it seemed that one could not walk more than a few paces without being obliged to stop, and make a small bow in gassho, before continuing. Small talk, which certainly included "annoying" questions asked by a visiting student, was frowned upon. But I was to discover far more major obstacles in the meditation hall (called the *zendo*). At first, I entered making random small bows, as seemed advisable, and made my way into the zendo proper.

I felt a hand on my shoulder stopping me as I was about to cross the threshold into the meditation hall. Turning, I faced what I took to be a monk (it wasn't, he was simply a lay member dressed in lay robes), frowning and wagging his finger at me. In a stage whisper he instructed me to return to the door and remove my shoes, placing them in one of the cubby holes in the structure next to the entrance. He then proceeded to instruct me in meaningful tones about the importance of entering the

Zendo with the with my left foot first as I step over the threshold. He also showed me how to walk in what he called *shashu* and indicated I really should be walking around in shashu most of the time.

He then kindly informed me that when I leave the Zendo I should be sure to step out with my right foot across the threshold. At first, I got these confused on a regular basis, and received numerous *"Tsk, tsk"* (*"Tut, tut"* for British readers) comments and frowning glances, with looks that seemed to say *"How on earth does he not get this?!"* In classic Zen fashion, such attention to needing to do everything "right" was coupled by people repeatedly telling me that everything is relaxed at the center, no one really minds if you don't do it right. Which is not how it felt to me. Over time, you do get used to it and it will depend on your personality whether you eventually find the formality and regimentation comforting, even stilling, or whether you continue to find it irritating. I was delighted to find I fell into the former camp. Zen might be for me.

Your experience at a more formal Zen center will be more complete than at a smaller sitting group: not just Zazen being sat in the Zendo, but dharma talks, dharma discussion, services with liturgy, incense burning, chanting, members attired in a variety of carefully color-coded items worn over robes, social time, and even communal lunches or gatherings with tea with cookies (homemade cookies have become a tradition in several American Zen centers, traditionally served with green tea). Such are the elements of Zen culture that you will soon become accustomed to.

A Day at a Zen Center

A full day of practice at a U.S. Soto Zen Center might begin with an early morning service. Resident monks and nuns may have been up at 4 a.m. to sit Zazen but visiting lay members will arrive at perhaps 8 a.m. for the service. The service will likely take place in a room devoted for such practice where there is an altar and an open arrangement to allow members to participate. On a larger campus, this will be one of four areas: the building or room where services take place (with a name like "Buddha Hall"), the zendo for sitting Zazen, a separate building or room for dharma talks (with a name like "Dharma Hall") and of course a main building where members meet and socialize (with a name like "Sangha House") which will have the main administrative offices in it.

I. Service and Liturgy: the Buddha Hall

If it is the first Japanese style Soto service you've attended, a couple of things may strike you. It will be very formal, with an almost military precision to the movements of the priests and monks presiding over the proceedings. The room is likely fairly empty, no pews or chairs to sit on, just an altar in the middle of the far wall. Then on the floor some feet in front of the altar will be a large flat cushion (*zabuton* Jp) to be used by the main presiding priest (*Doshi* Jp). You'll leave your shoes in the area just outside the main door, and file in one at a time being careful again to note which foot you put forward first over the threshold.

Once in, you and the other attendees will form a line around the edge of the room, backs to the walls, hands in *shashu*. Some monks or priests will be on cushions (*zafus*) on top of *zabutons*. In one corner will likely be the priest or monk designated to ring bells during the service (the *Doan*), one of which bells is likely to be the *inkin*, a small bell on top of a lacquered handle hit with a thin pin-like striker. In another corner will be someone known as the *fukodo* sitting in front of a large wooden drum in the shape of a fish—the *mokugo* (which means "wooden fish"). This will be used during the service to set a kind of heartbeat while attendees are chanting, keeping everyone in time.

Once the attendees are in place, the *Doshi* and other priests or helpers will process in. Their movements will be slow and deliberate, marking the solemnity of the proceedings. The order in which they enter, and the manner in which they enter, is all in accord with hierarchy and careful choreography. This group of people who serve in temple roles is known as the *doan-ryo* in the Soto tradition. Entering first may be the *kokyo*—the person who will be calling out the chant: a kind of cantor, if you are familiar with that term. Also entering first will be the *doan*, one who rings the bells, and may be in charge of lighting candles and preparing incense for the altar.

The service assistants enter single file and split off ahead of the *zabuton* in front of the altar, standing either side to the left and right. They bow to the altar in *gassho*, turn, bow to each other, then stand facing each other in *sasho*. Then the *jisha* enters, walking just in front of the *doshi*. The *jisha* is the assistant to the lead priest, the *doshi*, and it is their job to carry the incense offering, and hand it to the *doshi* at the altar at just the right moment. The *doshi* may be a head priest, or perhaps a Zen Master or the abbot. They may also be a *roshi*—which

12

literally means "old teacher." In the West, the term *roshi* has become mistakenly confused with "Zen Master" when in fact in Japan it is a title of respect given to older teachers. Here in the West it is usually reserved only for those who have received "final transmission" or, in Japanese, *inka shomei*.

The *jisha* holds an inkin; a bell on a handle in one hand, and a striker in the other. He will ring the bell to signal events such as the bowing of the *doshi*. Having rung the bell, he puts it down and picks up a stick of incense, and he or she then walks in parallel with the *doshi* to the altar. Their movements carefully synchronized. The *doshi* stops to the left of the altar and side steps, crab like, to be in the center. The *jisha* is holding the stick of incense using the fingers of both hands, held at chest height. When the *doshi* is ready to receive the incense, the *jisha* hands it to the *doshi* using his or her left hand, while holding the right hand up in one-handed *gassho*. The *doshi* places the lit incense stick into the center of a small pot with fine sand in it. The stick is carefully placed in the absolute center, perfectly vertical. She then picks a pinch of powdered incense and lifts it to her forehead, which is gently bowed, before placing it on top of some charcoal embers in another small pot. A second pinch of the incense is then placed.

The *doshi* walks right (enters left, leaves right) from the altar back to in front of his *zabuton*, with the *jisha* following just behind, ending in his place behind the *doshi*. The *doshi* and all priests present lay down their ceremonial cloths (*zagu*) on the floor or mat in front of them. They fold it so that the white area forms a precise cross shape. The assigned person rings the *inkin* once, and the priests do a deep bow on their *zagu*, forehead to the floor, hands raise up slightly three times as if brushing something away from by their ears. The attendees either do this too on the floor in front of them or do a "standing bow." The *jisha* rings again, a second full bow. The *jisha* now rings twice, indicating it is the third and final bow.

This highly formalized, carefully coordinated series of events and actions is just the start of the service. I have presented it in some detail to convey an idea of what it will be like for you to attend such a service for the first time. It will continue with chanting interspersed with slight bows in *gassho* and at least one further set of three deep bows. The chant may be in English (or the local language), or in the Soto tradition it may be in Japanese. In a Japanese style Soto Zen service, the chant will likely be the *Heart Sutra* which is a key text for Zen Buddhists. Also chanted may be a dedication and The Four Vows.

By this point, particularly if you have a background of going to church, you may feel that Zen services have something in common with "High Church" liturgy, like that of the Catholic, Episcopalian or Lutheran faiths. All have altars, Christian churches have "smells and bells," too, and it may seem that the Buddhists are worshiping Buddha since his image is on the altar. But any similarity is misleading: in Zen, indeed in most of Buddhism, there is no worship of the Buddha, and that is not the reason his likeness is on the altar. There is acknowledgement of and reverence to the Buddha (as one of the three treasures—Buddha, Dharma, Sangha), but not worship of Buddha as any form of higher being or deity. That said, it may be of interest to quickly review some key texts that may be chanted in a Zen service.

Heart of Great Perfect Wisdom Sutra

Also known simply as the "Heart Sutra" (*Maka hannya haramitta shingyo*, Jp), this text is one of the most often recited at Zen centers:

Avalokiteshvara Bodhisattva, when deeply practicing prajna paramita, clearly saw that all five aggregates are empty and thus relieved all suff'ring. Shariputra, form does not differ from sunyata,[1] sunyata does not differ from form. Form itself is sunyata, sunyata itself form. Sensations, perceptions, formations, and consciousness are also like this. Shariputra, all dharmas are marked by emptiness; they neither arise nor cease, are neither defiled nor pure, neither increase nor decrease. Therefore, given emptiness, there is no form, no sensation, no perception, no formation, no consciousness; no eyes, no ears, no nose, no tongue, no body, no mind; no sight, no sound, no smell, no taste, no touch, no object of mind; no realm of sight; no realm of mind consciousness. There is neither ignorance nor extinction of ignorance neither old age and death, nor extinction of old age and death; no suff'ring, no cause, no cessation, no path; no knowledge and no attainment. With nothing to attain, a bodhisattva relies on prajna paramita and thus the mind is without hindrance. Without hindrance, there is no fear. Far beyond all inverted views, one realizes nirvana. All buddhas of past, present, and future rely on prajna paramita and thereby attain unsurpassed, complete, perfect awakening. Therefore, know the prajna paramita as the great miraculous mantra, the great bright mantra, the supreme mantra, the incomparable mantra, which removes all suff'ring and is true, not false.

*Therefore, we proclaim the prajna paramita mantra, the mantra
that says:*
Gate Gate Paragate Parasamgate Bodhi Svaha
Gate Gate Paragate Parasamgate Bodhi Svaha
Gate Gate Paragate Parasamgate Bodhi Svaha

This single text concisely summarizes the core teachings of Zen Buddhism. If you come from a churched background, you will find the way it is chanted quite unusual. It is chanted to the fairly swift rhythm of the drum being struck (the *mokugyo*), in a monotone with hardly a breath taken between words. Accomplished practitioners have memorized it (although not everyone is gifted with the ability to memorize) and seem to chant it all without taking a breath. The ending translates to: *"Gone, gone, gone over, gone fully over. Awaken! So be it!"*

Dedication (*Ji ho san shi*, Jp)

> *All buddhas throughout space and time,*
> *All honored ones, bodhisattvas, mahasattvas,*
> *Wisdom beyond wisdom, maha-prajnaparamita.*

Then toward the end of the service, you will likely chant the four vows that are also central to Zen practice:

The Four Vows (*Shigu seigan mon*, Jp)

> *Sentient beings are numberless; I vow to save them.*
> *Desires are inexhaustible; I vow to end them.*
> *The Dharma Gates are infinite; I vow to enter them all.*
> *The Buddha Way is unattainable; I vow to attain it.*

I mentioned earlier Zen's penchant for contradictory language, and this is nowhere clearer than in the four vows. At first glance, indeed on repeated glances, these vows may seem nonsensical. If there are numberless beings, how can I vow to save them all? Shouldn't it be "I vow to save as many of them as I can"? No, this wording is there for a reason, much like the contradictory or puzzling language found in Zen koans. The same for desires being inexhaustible and yet you are vowing to end them, and the dharma gates (ways to discover The Truth, or your True Self) are infinite yet you are vowing to enter them all, and the Buddha Way is unattainable and yet you are vowing to attain it. How can this be so? Zen calls for a lot of trust—in Zen it is called "Great Faith"—that while this may all seem nonsensical to you at first, in time it will make perfect sense.

The Zendo: The Meditation Hall

From the service you will then join a line, single file, walking slowly in *shashu* to the zendo, or meditation hall. You'll soon see that whenever you walk anywhere on the Zen center campus, you will do so in *shashu*, and if you are wearing a *rakusu* then your hands are in *shashu* behind it. At the entrance of the zendo you will note that everyone is taking off their shoes, and that there will be an area for storing shoes. It is quite usual for people to also leave their car keys and other bulky items in their shoes to be maximally comfortable while meditating.

If this is a Japanese style Soto center, then you will see that all attendees are either wearing black robes, or black *samue* jackets, or wearing black (or dark color) clothing. Yoga style clothing is popular since it is loose-fitting and thus comfortable to wear for extended meditation sessions. You may find that wearing "regular" street clothes, especially shorts or jeans, is frowned upon or even forbidden in the zendo. The same may apply to t-shirts with slogans or pictures on them, with plain t-shirts being favored.

You may also have noticed by this point that people are wearing different color *rakusus* (like a bib, worn round the neck) and that the priests and teachers are wearing an additional second layer of robes instead of a *rakusu*. What this all means will vary from one Zen center to another, depending on what we call their "lineage"—how the transmission of teaching or priesthood was made from which person to which person and within which branch of the tradition.

But, for instance, people who have taken the precepts (an introductory start to more serious study in which one receives a "dharma name") will be wearing black *rakusus*. Priests may be wearing blue ones, and teachers may be wearing brown ones. The abbot, or *roshi*, may be wearing a more elaborate, colorful *rakusu*, or may be wearing a light sandy brown (ochre) outer "sheet robe" called a *kesa*. Some priests may be wearing black *kesas*, and some teachers may be wearing brown ones. That said, in some Zen centers those who have just taken the precepts may be wearing blue *rakusus*, and the priests may be wearing black ones. Again, things differ center to center, lineage to lineage.

The *kesas* are the outer robes that go over left shoulder and under the right shoulder, with the surplus material of the robe hanging over the left arm.

You'll enter the zendo left foot first and walk in *shashu* to a cushion or chair. In some centers you will select a cushion from a store of them in the entryway and carry it to a *zabuton* at one of the sitting locations inside the zendo. It may be wise to check in with a seasoned member of the center, or with someone who may appear to be helping newcomers, to see where it would be acceptable for you to sit. Perhaps it is human nature, but you should not be surprised if certain spots are understood to be reserved for seasoned practitioners. And of course, you will not wish to sit where a key person is assigned to sit, such as the abbot, zendo assistants, or the timekeeper.

Depending on the layout of the zendo, you may also be discouraged from walking in front of the altar, or to at least perform a slight bow if you do need to walk past it. Having found your position, you will make a slight bow in *gassho* to the cushion (or chair), then turn to face the room and make another slight bow in *gassho*. If there is someone in front of you, it will be usual for them to reply with a bow in *gassho*, too. As people stand in front of their cushions or chairs, you may find they bow in gassho whenever anyone across from them does so. Zen can involve a copious amount of bowing.

Most Soto Zen centers will start by sitting facing the wall. Indeed, they may continue to sit only facing the wall for all sittings that day. In other centers, you may find they start by facing the wall and then turn to face into the room toward others. You may also witness those present who wear a *rakusu* are not wearing them at first, but then all put them on in unison as the Robe Verse is chanted some way into the service. The *rakusu* is worn by Zen Buddhists who have taken what we call the "precepts" (more about which later in this book). It is a miniature version of the Buddha's robes, and dates back to a practice established in the original Chinese *Chan* tradition (some may argue that it *is* the Buddha's robes, not merely a representation of it). You will see that initially they will place the folded *rakusu* on their head, holding their hands in *gassho*, and then as the robe chant happens, they carefully undo it and place it around their necks. Here is the **Robe Verse** (*Takkesa ge*, Jp):

> *Great robe of liberation, field far beyond form and emptiness*
> *Wearing the Tathagata's teaching, saving all beings*
> (usually said three times followed by a bow)

A usual schedule will include an initial period of sitting for about 40 minutes followed by a period of walking meditation, which is then followed by a final 40-minute sitting session. A bell will ring at the end of the first sitting period, and you will notice that everyone gets up (slowly if they have been sitting cross legged, to allow for the circulation to return), and they will brush off their cushions or chair seat. There is a bow in *gassho* to the seat, and then practitioners turn to the center of the room, standing in *gassho*. The timer will then use some wooden blocks ("clappers") to make a sound to indicate the start of the walking meditation (known as *kinhin*, Jp). You bow, switch to *Shashu* and turn a quarter turn counterclockwise. Your head slightly bowed, eyes looking about 45 degrees down, you start to walk very slowly.

The format can be different from center to center, but in many Soto centers you will walk like this, one step for each full breath, until the clappers sound again whereupon you start walking briskly. When the clappers sound a third time, you then continue walking briskly until you arrived back at your cushion or chair. You bow to your cushion, turn and bow to the room, and sit. You'll need to check whether for this session people are facing the wall or the room—in some cases the group switches to facing into the room once the *rakusus* have been put on after the Robe Verse is said.

Face to Face Interviews: *Dokusan* (Jp)

If you are attending a Rinzai or Korean Zen center, or a Soto Zen center that is in the Harada-Yasutani lineage, then you will likely have access to one-on-one sessions. The Sanbo Kyodan sect of Zen mixes the Soto (Caodong) and Rinzai (Linji) traditions of sitting zazen and having koan introspection. This branch of Zen is associated with its founder Hakuun Yasutani, who formed this hybrid branch in 1954 after splitting from the main Soto branch which based itself particularly on the teachings of Dogen Zenji who brought Soto Zen to Japan from China. It is often called the Harada-Yasutani school of Zen in honor of Yasutani's teacher, Harada Daiun Sogaku. This school of Zen changed its name to simply "Sanbo Zen" in 2014. An example of a Zen center in the Sanbo Zen tradition is Mountain Cloud Center in Santa Fe, New Mexico, headed up by Henry Shukman (Ryu'un-ken).

Some branches of the American Soto school of Zen have adopted this hybrid of zazen and koan work, notably the *White Plum Asanga* founded by Taizan Maezumi Roshi in the late 1960s. Notable White Plum centers include: Zen Center of Los Angeles; Yokoji Zen Mountain Center in Redlands, California; The Zen Center of New York City; and Upaya Zen Center in Santa Fe, New Mexico (however, Upaya has not customarily offered koan introspection).

If the center offers *dokusan* you will probably need to obtain guidance as to the center's protocol for such interviews. In some cases, all will be welcome to go to *dokusan*, in other cases only established students will be permitted, or at least given priority. Usually, some way into the first sitting period the head teacher will leave the zendo and head to their interview room. Shortly after a bell will ring which indicates to members that they may now come to line up for *dokusan*—usually somewhere outside the room the interviews take place in. In centers where there may be more people wishing *dokusan* than there is time for it to take place, a system may be devised to randomize who can take a turn that particular week.

For instance, at Zen Center of Los Angeles, the tradition is that either the "garden side" or the "street side" of the zendo will be called first. Once all members interested in *dokusan* from that side have finished, if there is time the other side will be summoned. While it may seem overly complex, it is likely that which side is called will be randomized so that members cannot "game the system" to always sit on the side that will be called first each week.

Like most aspects of life at a Zen center, waiting in line for *dokusan* is scripted with rules to be carefully followed. Each person in line sits or kneels, and the person at the front of the line will hit a bell to let the teacher know they are about to enter the interview room. However, they do not hit the bell until they hear the teacher ring his or her bell, which is the sign that he or she has ended the session with the prior student. To be done "right," the incoming student needs to walk to the door of the teacher's room as the prior student is leaving, so as to enter just after the prior student exits. Protocol often calls for the student entering to keep facing the teacher as they enter, closing the door behind them.

A small bow at first, the student entering in *gassho* then does a full prostration (deep bow) on the *zabuton* in front of the teacher. The student then reaches for a nearby cushion to sit on during the interview or kneels on the *zabuton*. While different teachers have different requirements, it will not be unusual for a teacher to require strict formal adherence to placing the hands in *gassho* while stating their name and their "practice." Often the practice will be the koan they are working on. Hence, "*My name is Myoko and my practice is the koan Mu.*"

Some teachers will then be silent and expect the student to present their latest response to the koan, other teachers will say something like, "Are you here to present to me on this koan?" What the student does or says next will determine whether this *dokusan* session will last seconds or minutes. For instance, if the teacher is trying to encourage the student to give a non-verbal response to the koan, then the moment the student utters any sound the teacher will ring the bell, signaling the end of the session.

In this form of Soto koan work, like many Rinzai teachers, the Soto teacher will not enter into extended conversations with the student. At most the session will usually last a few minutes and may last just a few seconds. Although it is not a practice I condone, some teachers will swipe at the student with a small stick if they give a wrong answer. Given there is often a lack of opportunity for the teacher to get to know the student outside of these brief *dokusan* encounters, it seems unwise to assume that the student does not suffer some historic trauma that would be invoked by a sudden hit with a stick. I'll return to the topic of koans later.

Following the zazen session there may be a brief tea break in the center's communal area (perhaps known as the "Sangha House" or similar). Zen practitioners are renown for drinking herbal tea and eating home made cookies, although some centers will also offer coffee and cold drinks, too. You may find your fellow center visitors and members are fairly subdued during this time, partly because they are relaxed following zazen and thus not in the mood to "chat," and partly perhaps because Zen does seem to attract those more at the introvert end of the spectrum. What you will not find is anyone usually discussing Zen, and certainly not discussing their koan work in *dokusan*. If no one has explicitly told you this is taboo, you will have gathered that fact fairly early on in some way or another.

After the break members may then head over to the room or building designated for talks (perhaps with a name like Dharma Hall), to listen to a Zen teacher give a talk. While again there is no set format for such talks, usually this space will be laid out with rows of chairs, and perhaps a few people sitting on cushions toward the front. In the front will be a *zabuton* and *zafu* on which the teacher will sit, with a small lectern on which the teacher will keep their notes for the talk.

If this is a formal talk by a senior teacher, or by the *Roshi*, especially if it is based on a koan, then the talk may be referred to as a *teisho* (Jp). The distinction being that some say technically a *teisho* is a non-dualistic presentation, whereas a dharma talk is a lecture on a Buddhism theme or topic. There is complete silence during the talk, following which the speaker may then take questions. You will notice that several of the monks and priests may have taken their more formal robes off for this talk and instead donned their *rakusus*.

Following the talk, depending on the Center, there may then be a group (sangha) lunch where those who wish to can stay and socialize. What you may have noticed is that this day I have described covers all three of what Buddhism calls the "Three Jewels:" Buddha, Dharma and Sangha. It is no coincidence, then, that the day started with a service and zazen ("Buddha") moved on to a dharma talk ("Dharma") and ends with a period of socialization ("Sangha" or group).

Non-Japanese Zen Centers and Groups

So far, we have focused on mainly Japanese Zen centers, and mainly the Soto Zen centers since they are the most common in the United States and elsewhere in the West. But what of other kinds of Zen centers? Such as Korean or Vietnamese Zen centers for instance?

Vietnamese Zen

Probably the most famous Vietnamese Zen teacher is Thich Nhat Hanh, the highly popular writer and speaker who was mainly based at his center in southwest France, Plum Village Monastery, but who at the time of writing this book has now returned to his root temple in Vietnam to live out his final days. Thich Nhat Hanh is affectionately known as "Thay" (which means teacher—like all ordained Vietnamese Zen Buddhist priests and monks, I too technically have the title thay, but do not use it). Thay does not teach traditional Vietnamese Zen Buddhism. Rather, he teaches his own brand of Zen with some Pure Land Buddhist influence, focused on mindfulness and what he calls "Interbeing." Indeed, his school of Zen is known as the "Order of Interbeing."

Thay's order teaches what they call the "Five Mindfulness Trainings," and the "Fourteen Mindfulness Trainings." In the U.S. he established Deer Park Monastery in Escondido, Southern California, and Green Mountain Dharma Center in Vermont. Well known members of the Order of Interbeing include Natalie Goldberg, Larry Rosenberg, Cheri Marples, Jack Kornfield, and the comedian Gary Shandling. Others who were his students include Joan Halifax (who is now in the White Plum Asanga, and runs Upaya in New Mexico), and Jon Kabat-Zinn who developed "Mindfulness Based Stress Reduction."

If you attend one of the Order's centers, or meditation groups, you will not find a practice that is similar to either the Japanese Soto or Rinzai traditions (which have similarities to each other) or the Korean Zen tradition, which also has some similarities with the Japanese sects.

Although far less well known, the other major Vietnamese Zen teacher. was Thich Thien-An, who brought Zen to the U.S while in 1966 he was a visiting professor at the University of California, Los Angeles (UCLA). Thien-An taught traditional Thien meditation, that is, traditional Vietnamese Zen meditation ("Thien" being the Vietnamese pronunciation of the Chinese character Chan). Through the encouragement of his enthusiastic students, he founded the *International Buddhist Meditation Center* in Koreatown, Los Angeles, California in 1970.

Sadly he passed of liver cancer in 1980, but his Los Angeles center continues, and his teaching also continues through such other centers as the Desert Zen Center in Lucerne Valley, California, run by Thien-An's student, the Venerable Thich An Giao, Roshi. Thien-An's teachings are also continued by the Five Mountain Zen Center, founded by Venerable Wonji Dharma (Paul Lynch), which also teaches in the Korean Zen tradition. I am ordained in this tradition.

Korean Zen

Korean Zen is known as Korean Seon—where Seon is the Korean pronunciation of the Chinese character for Chan. Korean Zen has a focus on koan work, largely because many Korean Zen sects grew out of the Chinese school of Zen founded by Linji Yixuan (known as Rinzai in Japan). In the U.S., Korean Zen was spread by the Zen Master Seung Sahn, who set up a wide network of centers known as the Kwan Um School of Zen.

Having first founded the Providence Zen Center in the early 1970s, he went on to found around 100 further Kwan Um centers in six continents. Seung Sahn was also known as Seonsanim, and later in life he was known as Daesoensanim from 1987 when he became sixty years old. He is famed for his brand of Zen teaching that includes phrases like "Only go straight," and "Only don't know." He referred to his teachings as "Don't Know Zen," reminiscent of the teachings of the founder of Zen, Bodhidharma. His teachings continue through a number of Kwan Um centers in the United States, and through the teachers in the Five Mountain Zen Order, founded by Venerable Wonji Dharma (Paul Lynch). I am ordained in this tradition, too.

What you will find in attending both Thay's Order of Interbeing centers and centers associated with the teachings of Seung Sahn, is they are more relaxed and easy going than their Japanese originated Soto Zen centers. For instance, some of these schools of Zen will not require that members wear specific clothing to mediate in, nor that they only wear somber dark colored clothing.

Perhaps one of the biggest differences between Korean Zen practice and that of Japanese Soto or Rinzai Zen, is that face to face interviews (*dokusan* in Japanese) can be more in the form of a casual conversation rather than a strictly controlled sessions that may be over in seconds, or at most minutes. Seung Sahn is famous for saying that such one-on-one interviews with a Korean Zen teacher can be about koan (Korean "kong-an") work, or they may be about current affairs and news, or how the student has been doing in the intervening week since the last session. The potential advantage of this approach is that students may progress faster in their koan work where there is a degree of friendly discussion, than in Soto or Rinzai where discussion is frowned upon. But, that said, each student should explore which method works best for them.

Obviously, there are differences of opinion on how best to work with a student on koans. Those from the Japanese tradition may argue that in order for a student to have a glimpse of awakening (a so-called *kensho* moment), it is necessary to jolt them into awareness, not slowly coax them into awareness with lengthy friendly discussion. That said, there is little evidence that being so strict with koan teaching leads to more swift self-realization or awakening. On the contrary, it is not unusual for those following the Japanese method to spend many years working on the same koan with little to no change in their awareness of who they truly are. That said, such lack of progress can happen in the more relaxed approach too, but there at least a student has support and mentorship perhaps lacking in the more rigid Soto/Rinzai method.

Korean Zen is also more associated with the use of what are known as "*huatou*" (*hwadu*, Korean; *wato*, Japanese), part of a meditation practice known as "Gongfu." This is more common to the Chinese Chan teachings, and those of the Korean Seon school and Rinzai Zen. *Huatou* means "word head" or the main head case of a koan. This can be a short word or phrase that helps focus the mind. Thus, rather than mediated or contemplate a lengthy koan (as might happen in the hybrid Soto tradition), in these schools the student meditates on a brief phrase that can be used even in the course of daily activities. This practice has its roots in the teaching of Dahui Zonggao, the famous Chinese Chan Master teaching in the Linji tradition.

Dahui lived from 1089-1163 C.E. and is one of the better-known Chinese Zen Masters. He focused on this teaching technique of *kan huatou* ("inspecting the critical phrase") and taught that lay people can become awakened using this technique. Dahui was a loud critic of the so-called "silent illumination" claims of the rival Caodong (Soto) school that emphasized the idea of becoming awakened solely by sitting zazen, facing a wall for years. Dahui felt that was a heretical claim.

Well known *huatou* include phrases such as "What is this?" (very popular in Korean Zen, with Seung Sahn adding "Don't know" afterwards), "Who am I?" and "Who is dragging this corpse around?" This method leads to an active form of meditation which is in stark contrast to the traditional forms of

Soto Zazen which leads some to see Zen as just a form of quietism.

In the Japanese based Soto schools in the U.S. that practice koan introspection, the koan Mu has been adopted as a form of *huatou*. Students are encouraged to repeat the word "Mu" to themselves on an ongoing basis, day in day out, sitting with Mu, diving deep into Mu, immersing themselves in Mu. For this reason, if you attend a Soto Zen center in the U.S. you may encounter students walking around saying "Mu"—often in a very deep resonant tone—and don't be surprised if when waiting for your turn at *dokusan* a resounding "Mu!" emerges from the interview room as the student ahead of you presents the koan.

The koan Mu is often used as the first that a student experiences in the Japanese Rinzai and Soto traditions. It goes like this:

> *A monk asked Zhaozhou Congshen, a Chinese Zen*
> *master (Joshu in Japanese), "Does a dog have Buddha-*
> *nature or not?" Zhaozhou responded "Wu" (Japanese*
> *"Mu").*

Wu (or Mu) means no, and for this reason some have mistakenly associated Joshu's response with *sunyata* (see endnote number 1). While we will never know, it may be possible given the humorous bent of some of the early Zen masters, that in Chinese the word "Wu" was selected because it both evokes the sound a dog makes ("woof")[2] and the concept of no. This koan remains in wide use within the Rinzai and Soto schools to encourage students to gain an initial insight into their Buddha-nature. Korean Zen teachers also use it.

However, by the 17th century, the Rinzai master Hakuin Ekaku had become annoyed by what he saw as stagnation in practice that arose from overuse of the koan Mu. He thus invented his own new starter koan which replaced Mu in his teaching curriculum. His koan is the well-known one that has entered popular culture, misquoted as "*What is the sound of one hand clapping?*" As mentioned above, the actual koan is "*Two hands clap and there is a sound. What is the sound of one hand?*"

While this may at first sight seem to be a quite different koan from "Mu" it is in fact a very similar koan. Realizing their similarity is part of what may enable a student to have a glimpse of their Buddha-nature, a glimpse of awakening. Hakuin used a well-known Buddhist term called the "great doubt" which a koan can cause by creating a tension that can lead to awakening. He said, "At the bottom of great doubt is great awakening. If you doubt completely, you awaken completely." This "great doubt," of course, is precisely what Master Seung Sahn addressed with his teaching to repeat to oneself, "What's this? Don't know."

Zen then is like chess: fairly simple to learn the basics, but it can take a lifetime of devotion to practice to fully embody the Buddha Way. You may wonder why I did not define Zen as being a way to become enlightened. Zen is full of contradictions, and one that you will come across is a clear implication that the ultimate goal of Zen is to "become enlightened" as well as reading that Zen has no goals. Worse, you will learn that no one "becomes enlightened" since, Zen teaches, you are already awake—you just need to realize that.

Enlightenment is a poor term that seasoned Zen teachers steer clear of. Rather, Zen speaks of *realizing* your true self, your Buddha-nature, or simply of awakening. In Zen we learn there is nothing to gain, nothing to attain. And yet, despite that, you will find Zen teachers and even Zen masters using wording that certainly sounds like there are levels of achievement, and goals to aim for. Such contradictory messages are part of Zen culture, so much so that you may be forgiven for wondering after a while if those who devised Zen had a rather impish sense of humor.

---

[1] Sunyata is often translated as "emptiness" or "voidness," but better translations might be "transparency" or "ground." Some say transparency has value and emptiness has none, and that Sunyata is the Ground upon which Form appears.

[2] Others have pointed out that the Chinese say the sound a dog makes is "wong, wong." It would be wise not to dwell overly much on this.

Not thinking about anything is Zen. Once you know this, walking, standing, sitting or lying down, everything is Zen.

Bodhidharma

two

Why Practice Zen?

The Dalai Lama has said that the main purpose of life is happiness. Many of us, though, would settle for a day with less stress in it than the prior day. The idea of being happy all the time may sound attractive, but few human beings see that as possible in their day to day lives. Indeed, a perpetual state of happiness—in the sense we usually mean that—invokes some kind of 1960s hippie concept. Walking around with a perpetual smile no matter how awful what is happening in the world may be does not sound a very balanced state to be in.

Indeed, Zen does not teach that our goal is to be happy, rather if this is a time for sadness (at, say the loss of a loved one), then be 100% sad. Enter fully into that sadness. If you have reason to be happy, then be 100% happy. Enter fully into that. Zen is about waking up to exactly who you are, which carries with it a full embodiment of all your emotions. But for most human beings accepting their emotions, or indeed fully embodying them, is not even on the radar as a key goal in life.

Rather, particularly in the West, we are very self-centered and see progress or success as measured by how much more one has achieved today than yesterday. We come from a position of seeing ourselves as less than perfect, less than what we could be, and reject our ability to have self-awareness—which is sad since it is one of our greatest gifts. Instead, we focus on "improving" ourselves or our situation. But what if I told you that you are perfect just as you are (although you could use some improvement, as Zen master Shunryu Suzuki said)? You would probably call me mad.

We're forever looking outside of ourselves for solutions that will make us feel better, feel more perfect. If only we had a better job, if only we had more money, if only we knew the right people. If we look to ourselves at all, then it is for some societal based goal such as, "If only I could be slimmer," or, "If only my muscles were more toned." Yes, we may have worthy goals such as seeking to be healthier, but rarely is seeking health seen as a main human goal. We always want more.

Yet, the fact you are reading this book probably means you sense something deeper. You perhaps sense that beyond all these petty human selfish goals or greater wealth and social standing is a more important truth: that you are deep down limitless and boundless. That there is no limit to your potential, but something is persistently getting in the way of you seeing how to realize this deeper truth.

For many of us realization starts to dawn as we get older, for some it can come earlier in life. We have switched jobs and found we are still lacking something. The job seemed to be what was holding us back from achieving our true goal, but no matter how many job changes it always seems unsatisfying. Or perhaps you are lucky enough to have a major promotion with a sizable increase in salary, yet still you don't feel satisfied. With greater income comes society's pressure to want more, almost as if no matter how much you earn it would never be sufficient. Indeed, if you are looking for this deeper sense of achieving a core life goal, it will never come from these external achievements. And perhaps that has dawned on you by this point, hence you are exploring Zen.

You have maybe run down your many lists of "If only I could ..." and come to the conclusion that none of these goals actually left you feeling more satisfied, more whole. Of course, if you're not careful, Zen can bring a whole new list of "If only" possibilities. If only I could sit full lotus. If only I could sit more upright, more still like she does. If only I could work out what awakening is. If only I could do my precepts. If only I could wear monk robes. If only I could become a fully ordained Zen monk or priest—the temptation to find what you are looking for out there in titles and so-called achievements has the potential to dog you in Zen as it has dogged you in the rest of your life.

Although it can be very hard to appreciate, the problems you perceive arise mainly from your belief that you are a person in a world full of entirely separate, independent other people. You are essentially a thing, an object, defined by various societal labels and norms. When you meet strangers in a social gathering, it's likely initial questions involve ones such as "What do you do for a living?" or "What part of town do you live in?" or "Have you lived here long?" or "How do you know the host of this event?"

Inherent in such questions are concepts that define you in relation to these labels and definitions that society—other people—have decided are what define you. Thus, in response to your saying what you do for a living, the other person may privately think, or even say out loud, "Oh that, I could never live on the wage that job gives." Or, "Oh that part of town, isn't it rather dangerous?" Or perhaps, "Oh you know a friend of the host, well I know the host himself." Even when there is a sincere attempt not to judge and compare, still judgment and comparison happens daily in many of our social interactions. And they subtly help form your view of "who you are" as defined by all these external measures.

What is central to all this of course is the idea that you are a separate individual, limited, struggling to be a better individual, to be more successful as an individual. But this also means that whether you feel good, whether you suffer, whether you are lifted up or put down, is all in the hands of others "out there." The ways this mode of thinking can corrupt us are endless. It can lead to a way of thinking that is driven by "What is in it for me?" rather than "How will this benefit others?"

So, we get a better job so that *we* benefit, not others. So that *we* get more money, not others. To this part many of you may be thinking, "Well, of course! Why wouldn't I want to benefit from what I achieve in life?" But that is the narrow view we all get sucked into: the view of ourselves as an object that can become a better object. And that all we need to be concerned with is how *this* object (person) is doing, no regard for others since whether they fail or succeed is entirely up to them. What we fail to see is this mode of thinking is *precisely* our main problem. It is dualistic thinking that can only result in suffering.

We thus turn to a spiritual path to address our need to better ourselves, or to seek a deep personal peace or happiness. Will Zen give that to you? The more familiar you become with Zen, the more you will come to expect answers that are contradictory. These questions—of whether a spiritual path will give you certain results—are examples of what in Zen are called "gaining mind." That is, goals and expectations that you are going to gain something from this practice.

In fact, this practice is about letting everything drop away, rather than gaining anything. I mentioned earlier that the term "enlightenment" is not well-liked in Zen circles since it implies something you gain. The common phrase is "to become enlightened" which is almost the polar opposite of what Zen practice and teaching is all about. As confounding as it may sound, you are already awakened you merely have to realize that by becoming fully awake to your true self, your Buddha-nature.

Following the path of Zen is not for the faint hearted: it takes dedication and discipline. It turns out that it is surprisingly hard to achieve something that is both fundamentally simple and straightforward, and yet cannot be gained by achievement. Much like learning to ride a bicycle, listening to talks, watching videos, reading books, will only get you so far: to walk this path you will need to devote yourself to it since only you can awaken yourself, no one can awaken you for you.

Thus, whether you choose to pursue zazen as your practice, or koan introspection, or a mixture of the two, you will need courage to devote yourself fully. This is not a path that you pursue for a few weeks or months and expect a "result." Again, that is gaining mind. This Zen way calls for a commitment of years, perhaps the entirety of your adult life. The wonderful flipside of this is that the practice becomes your entire life, and it will be a life fully lived in a way that you likely cannot achieve by virtually any other practice.

There will be ups and downs: there will be times when you may feel on top of the world. You find a deep inner peace, and everything feels particularly right with the world. Then, without warning, perhaps things will feel as grey as grey can be, with a sense that you have practiced for years but gotten nowhere (this is technically true, of course, but that doesn't mean it can't be perceived as quite depressing). It is another Zen conundrum that while what you think of as your "ego" is illusionary, it can be this ego that leads to the highs and lows. Perhaps clearly, perhaps subtly, the feeling that *"I've made it! I'm a spiritual being with all this Zen work! I am one with everything! I get it!"* can creep in and rewards you with a sense of ecstasy. Yet on other days the ego will chide you with, *"Really? After all these years of sitting and doing koans, this is what you have to show for it? Pain when you sit, and nothing but frustration when you work on koans?"*

It's gaining mind again: you'll continue to meet this on your path. *"I thought I would gain something, and I have!"* (the high), *"I'm just not gaining anything from this practice"* (the low). Perhaps the feelings won't present themselves quite like this, indeed in Zen practice it tends to be subtle variations of such feelings that mean it will take courage, discipline and devotion.

three

A Brief History of Zen

Buddhism has its roots roughly 2,500 years ago in India with a man who woke up. Siddhartha Gautama (Siddhattha Gotama in *Pali*) is also known as Shakyamuni Buddha, the Great Sage of the Shakya clan. We believe his family name was Gautama and Siddhartha was his given name. Buddha is a title given to him, and simply means "Awakened One." He also referred to himself as "Tathagata" in the early writings known as the Pail Canon. This means "one who has thus come" and is believed to refer to his transcendent state of consciousness.

We know approximately when he lived—around 500 B.C.E.—but the precise dating of his birth and death is debated. Insofar as there is any consensus, historians have settled on his dates being 563 B.C.E. to 483 B.C.E. But other scholars claim archaeological evidence places his birth around 480 B.C.E. and his death around 400 B.C.E. According to legend he was born into a royal family in the region now known as Nepal. However, while he is referred to as a prince, and his father and mother as king and queen, it is unlikely they held titles of the kind we think of when we hear these words in the West.

His father was probably a leader in the Shakya clan, which was not one of the most highly regarded clans of that region in the 5th century before the common era. We have no surviving texts from his lifetime—some of the earliest date from around 250 B.C.E. when we get the "*Edicts of Ashoka*." These texts refer to the Buddha and to the village of Lumbini (in modern day Nepal) as his birthplace. And it is here that we first find him referred to as the Sage of the Shakya clan.

Trying to find factual information about the Buddha's life is almost impossible since as with other well know religious figures, after he died people raised him up to an almost god-like status, inventing events that elevate Buddha's life and acts to mythical proportions. In fact, we have every reason to believe he was a regular human being like any of us, but someone who both had a life transforming realization and had the aptitude to teach others about it.

As I discuss in my book on Christ and Buddha (*Christ Way, Buddha Way: Jesus as Wisdom Teacher and a Zen Perspective on His Teachings*), both Christ and Buddha were pedestalized. Indeed, there are strong similarities in their invented life stories such as both having miraculous births, both births being predicted by wise people, both being born of a virgin who had a miraculous pregnancy, and so on.

According to legend, Siddhartha was born into a life of privilege, whether as an actual prince or as the favored son of a community leader. The story describes how his overly protective father kept Siddhartha from knowing the world outside of the palace. We are to believe for instance that the royal gardeners were instructed to clip off any blooms from flowers that were fading so that Siddhartha would be protected from witnessing decay or death.

According to these same stories his father marries Siddhartha to a neighboring king's daughter, and ensures the couple are restricted to living in pleasure palaces where they cannot see the suffering of this world. Then, at around 29 years of age, Siddhartha finally gets to venture out of the palace compound into the outside world. First, he sees someone bent over in pain, coughing badly and burning up with a fever. He asks the servant accompanying what this is and is told it is known as "sickness." As they continue their journey Siddhartha then sees his first examples of old age and death. Finally, in the fourth of his visions he meets a homeless man who despite being poorly dressed seems at peace and happy.

He asks this ascetic—since from the stories that is clearly who it was—how he can be so peaceful and the ascetic tells him that he has decide to given up the life of living in a house with a wife in order to pursue a way out of the suffering of the world. On speaking with this homeless seeker after truth he knew he was called to do the same. He thus abandons his life as a royal prince and sets out to seek a way to overcome suffering arising from sickness, old age and death.

Siddhartha then spends the next six years living with ascetics who engaged in very strict practices. This began what became known as the 6-year fast. Eventually he assesses himself and decides that in his weakened state his thinking is far less clear than before the fasting, and that he is thus further from his goal than when he started six years earlier. Consequently, he decided to follow a middle way—indeed to this day Buddhism is known as the Middle Way—where he struck a balance between not indulging himself and not depriving himself.

Around this time Buddha found a fig tree that became known as the Bodhi Tree (a *Ficus religiosa*, the "tree of awakening"). He was determined to sit there under the tree until he realized the Truth he was seeking. He sat there for around 40 days and the temptress Mara tempted him in any way she could to stop him reaching full realization—full awakening. By the way, this has a parallel to the story of Jesus who on having his awakening experience while being baptized by John, then goes into the desert where he fasts for 40 days and is tempted by the devil. As I discuss in my book on Christ and Buddha, there are numerous parallels like this in the lives of Christ and Buddha.

It was the night of the full moon of the fourth Indian month (likely to be May or June in our calendar) when Siddhartha's meditation went to a new deeper level of concentration and as the sun was rising that morning he reputedly attained full awakening. In that moment, we are told, he became the Awakened One, the Buddha. Of course, Zen teaches us that he was always awake, always Buddha, just as you and I are.

He remained in the area of the Bodhi tree for around seven weeks before deciding to start teaching others. A fundamental element of his realization was that anyone who awakens is called to teach others—*to turn the dharma wheel* as we say in Buddhist parlance. He went on to live to around 80 years of age and developed his body of teaching that includes the Four Nobel Truths and the Eightfold Path. During his lifetime the foundations of a religious movement were started by Buddha and his followers, and the movement grew after his passing.

Around two hundred years later Ashoka the Great, the Mauryan Indian emperor, established Buddhism as the national religion in India. Under his guidance, numerous Buddhist monasteries were built, and he sent out emissaries far and wide to spread Buddhism, particularly west to the Middle East. Ashoka had particular success spreading Buddhism to the Hellenistic world, such that by around 250 B.C.E. there were many tens of thousands of Greek Buddhists. I discuss this in some depth in my book, *Christ Way, Buddha Way*.

Flash forward a few hundred years and Buddhism has been spreading throughout the Middle East and the East. On to the scene came a Buddhist monk name Bodhidharma who is said to have brought *dhyana* (Chan/Zen) to China about the 5th century C.E. We know very little about him other than that he was described by the Chinese as being "The Blue-Eyed Barbarian" who is said to have come from a Western region—which Western region, though, is unclear in the historic literature.

He is described as being a wide-eyed person not from China, who had a bushy red beard and blue eyes. Some accept that Bodhidharma was a real historical figure, others hold that he was a mythical figure invented as part of rewriting the early history of Zen. But if he had both blue eyes and red hair, then he was one of those rare human beings with both. Blue eyes and red hair are both recessive genes, and for someone to have both characteristics then both of their parents would have had to have both genes.

Most likely he came from one of the regions that was well known for having people with both red hair and blue eyes since otherwise it is statistically unlikely he had these attributes by sheer chance (only around 0.17% of people in the world have both blue eyes and red hair). However, if indeed he was a real person, it is perhaps not a mystery who Bodhidharma was and where he came from. The Yue-Chi (Yuezhi) peoples lived in Western China at the time Bodhidharma is said to have arrived in the Wei Province in North Eastern China, and the Yue-Chi had subjugated the local people who were known as the Wusun. The Wusun thus became intermingled with the conquering Yue-Chi.

The Wusun were renown as people who had both blue eyes and red hair—and they were particularly well known for having large red beards. The connection to Buddhism becomes clear when one realizes that Yue-Chi is the Chinese name for the central Asiatic tribe known as the Kush (or Kushans). This same tribe ruled Bactria and India in the early first century C.E. and its emperor Kanishka was well known to be a patron of Buddhism and that he is known to have spread Buddhism to the Indian subcontinent as well as Central Asia and China. This area of Bactria is precisely where the high population of Greek Buddhists was based. Indeed, the Kushans inherited the culture of the Greek Buddhist kingdom they replaced.[3]

While the Kushan empire itself was essentially replaced by the fourth century C.E., numerous Greco-Buddhist and Kushan Buddhist centers had already been established in the region. By this time the Kushan Buddhists had brought Buddhism to areas of North Western China, but more important the Kushans were well known to be fluent in the Chinese language and Chinese culture. It thus makes sense that Bodhidharma was one of these Kushan (Yue-Chi or Wusun) Buddhists, a number of whom were well known to have both blue eyes and red hair. They were also well known to have features quite different from the main Chinese population—which fits with how they described Bodhidharma. As historian S.G Goodrich reports:

> *The Wusun are first noticed in the third century B.C.E., as commingled with the Yue-Chi, on the north western confines of China proper. They differed entirely from their neighbors in personal appearance, and Chinese writers describe them as having blue eyes and a red beard.*[4]

In early Chan texts he is described as teaching in the Northern Wei territory,[5] which is on the eastern side of China, directly across from where the Kushan Buddhists first introduced Buddhism in North Western China. Given all these facts, including the explanation of his unique physical description, and his roots in the region that spread to China from the Greco-Buddhist world, this theory of who Bodhidharma was fits the facts far better than the traditional story that he was a royal prince from India.

That said, because Bodhidharma has become an almost semi-mythical character, there is great uncertainty whether he really existed and if so when he first came to China. Some accounts have him arriving in Southern China toward the end of the 5th century, and other records suggest he arrived during the next Chinese dynasty in the early 6th century. One of the first recorded events is a famous meeting between Bodhidharma and the Emperor Wu. The exchange is said to have gone like this:

> Emperor Wu: "How much karmic merit have I earned for ordaining Buddhist monks, building monasteries, having sutras copied, and commissioning Buddha images?"
> Bodhidharma: "None. Good deeds done with worldly intent bring good karma, but no merit."
> Emperor Wu: "So what is the highest meaning of noble truth?"
> Bodhidharma: "There is no noble truth, there is only emptiness."
> Emperor Wu: "Then, who is standing before me?"
> Bodhidharma: "Don't know, Your Majesty.[6]

This early quote immediately echoes a key teaching of Zen, "don't know"—beginner's mind is here at the start of Bodhidharma teachings. What he supposedly brought to

China is the Indian Buddhist teaching of meditation, *dhyana* in Sanskrit. The Chinese could not pronounce the Indian syllable *dhy*, and *dhyana* became transliterated at first as *chana*, which became *Chan*. When Chan spread to other countries, such as Korea and Japan, the same written character is pronounced differently: so, in Japan the same character is pronounced *Zen*, in Korea it is *Seon*, and in Vietnam it is pronounced *Thien*.

Failing to make a good impression in Southern China, he reputedly goes north to the Shaolin Temple in the Northern Territory. Some versions have him founding the Shaolin Temple (later famous for its martial arts monks and Kung Fu), other versions have it already established. According to one telling, he was denied entry to the temple and sat in a nearby cave, spending nine years wall-gazing. Some legends have him cutting off his own eye lids around the seventh year to help himself not fall asleep!

After nine years, the story goes that he was allowed to enter the temple and taught there for several years. Other stories say that after nine years of wall-gazing his legs atrophied and that this is why *Daruma dolls* have no legs (Daruma dolls being likenesses of Bodhidharma that are usually round and hollow, being essentially just a face and body showing his red beard). Such dolls are regarded as good luck charms, although are not formally part of Buddhist tradition.

Ultimately it is unclear there ever was someone named Bodhidharma, although there is some historical support for such a red bearded, blue-eyed monk being among those who introduced *dhyana* to China. However, that may have taken place a long time before the stories say it did since we have historical evidence that the Kushan empire sent such Buddhist monks to spread Buddhism to China in the first to second century—which is when Buddhism was first spread to China. The character of Bodhidharma may have been invented sometime in the 6th or 7th century to legitimize the Chan school of Buddhism in China.

It is central to Zen teaching, though, that historical events don't matter. As Korean Zen master Kusan told his students, their truth does not depend on whether Bodhidharma or any other Buddhist of history actually existed or not. From early on Zen (Chan) distanced itself from the study of sutras, and for many students this is one of its attractions. The focus is on seeing into one's own nature, not in "understanding" texts. While we may never know if he actually said it, a foundational quote relating to this idea attributed to Bodhidharma goes as follows:

A special transmission outside the scriptures
Not founded upon words and letters;
By pointing directly to one's mind
It lets one see into one's own true nature and thus attain
Buddhahood

By the 7th or 8th centuries, Chan had become very popular in China, but its critics dismissed it as not being a legitimate branch of Buddhism since it had no direct transmission that could be traced back to Buddha himself. While this may be true, it was a somewhat naïve criticism given that by the 7th century it would not have truly been difficult for anyone to trace their lineage back to Siddhartha Gautama. Some speculate, then, that around this time the character of

Bodhidharma was invented to help give legitimacy to the Chan tradition.

This push toward legitimizing Chan Buddhism culminated around 1000 C.E. with the publication of *The Jingde Record of the Transmission of the Lamp* (here I'll sometimes refer to it simply as *The Lamp*). This substantial 30 volume work contains the life stories of all the Zen ancestors—that is, all the main teachers in the Zen (Chan) lineage, all the way back to Buddha. In fact, it goes one better and goes back to before Siddhartha Gautama, and states that he was in fact the 7th Buddha, not the first! By the way, western literature tends to call these historic persons "patriarchs" but since Chinese is largely a gender-neutral language, "ancestors" is a more accurate term to use.

As to why the writer of *The Lamp* decided to have six Buddhas prior to Siddhartha is unclear. It may relate to the fact Buddhism arose in large part out of Jainism, and by Siddhartha's time there had supposedly already been twenty four main teachers, called *tirthankara,* and the 24th, *Mahavira,* was a contemporary of Buddha (he would have been about 25 years older than Buddha). The idea may have been based on the likely fact Buddha had *Mahavira* as one of his teachers, which would suggest there were awakened ones prior to Siddhartha's awakening.

As to where they came up with the idea that Siddhartha was the seventh Buddha, we don't know, but in the 7th century C.E. they may not have known that *Mahavira* was the 24th *tirthankara* since only modern scholarship has revealed that. Along with asserting Bodhidharma as the first ancestor of the Chinese Chan Buddhist tradition, it was of course important to them to establish who his immediate predecessor was. And they decided it was an Indian sage known as *Prajnatara*.

The problem is that outside of *The Lamp* there is little evidence that Prajnatara existed. Worse, *The Lamp* also asserts that Bohdidharma was the third son of an Indian Brahman King, and hailed from Southern India. But there is no evidence that is true, and as we have seen above, there is far more evidence that if he existed, he was probably a Buddhist monk with Wusun heritage. No one from Southern India would be described as having a bushy red beard and blue eyes, nor would they be described (as happens in the earliest texts) as coming from the western edge of China—which is where Wusun was.

One of the benefits of this invention of a legitimate foundation for Chan Buddhism, is that we have some choice teachings that are attributed either to Bodhidharma or his teacher. Here is a famous one attributed to his teacher:

> *The Venerable Prajnatara asks Bodhidharma, "What is it that is formless amongst things?"*
> *Bodhidharma says, "Formlessness is unborn."*
> *Prajnatara asks, "What is the highest amongst things?"*
> *Bodhidharma says, "The Actual Nature is the highest."*

Legend has it that Bodhidharma passed transmission to Dazu Huike (Taiso Eka, Jp; maybe 487-593 C.E.) who gained his position as the successor in a colorful manner. According to the famous text the *Gateless Gate*, Huike waited outside Bodhidharma's cave for many days in very inclement weather. He begged Bodhidharma to teach him and having got nowhere with his efforts eventually cut off his own arm to show how sincere he was. Apparently, historians later found that he had lost his arm to some wandering vagabonds and had impressed everyone by how calm he remained. Whatever actually happened, it seems Bodhidharma gave in and accepted him as a student. We gather that Huike had his great awakening as a result of the following exchange:

> Huike said to Bodhidharma, "My mind is anxious. Please pacify it."
> Bodhidharma replied, "Bring me your mind, and I will pacify it."
> Huike said, "Although I've sought it, I cannot find it."
> "There," Bodhidharma replied, "I have pacified your mind."

The next ancestors in the Chan lineage are supposedly Sengcan (Seng-ts'an, Jp), Daoxin (Doshin, Jp), Hongren (Konin, Jp), and Huineng (Daikan Eno, Jp). Once again, we know very little about these teachers, and much of what is attributed to them is of questionable provenance. That said, Sengcan is said to be the author of a famous Chinese poem *Faith in Mind*:

> *The Great Way is not difficult for those who have no preferences. When love and hate are both absent everything becomes clear and undisguised. Make the smallest distinction, however, and heaven and earth are set infinitely apart. If you wish to see the truth then hold no opinion for or against. The Struggle of what one likes and what one dislikes is the disease of the mind.*

The opening of this famous quote is reminiscent of Daoist teaching at the start of the famous *Daode Jing* (sometimes called *Tao te Ching*) by Laozi (also known as Lao Tzu):

The way that can be named is not the eternal way.

While some push back at the idea that Zen is the culmination of Indian Buddhist teaching mixing with the traditional Chinese Daoist philosophy, there are clear indications from early texts that from the beginning the Chinese teachers were synthesizing a new "way" by blending teachings from the two traditions. Indeed, we have good reason to believe the Chinese had issues with some of the Indian concepts and quite naturally processed them in the context of their national philosophy of Daoism. They undoubtedly saw parallels between the ideas expressed in Buddhist texts and Daoist ones. Again, this would have been Daoist *philosophy*, not Daoist pantheistic *religion* that involves various superstitions, ritual sacrifices, etc.

The next patriarch Daoxin (Dao-hsin) literally has a connection with traditional Daoist philosophy in his name. This is a reputed conversation in the *Compendium of Five Lamps* (attributed to Sengcan) when Daoxin was 14 years old:

Daoxin: I ask for the Master's compassion. Please instruct me on how to achieve release.
Sengcan: Is there someone who constrains [binds] you?
Daoxin: There is no such person.
Sengcan: Why then seek release when you are constrained by no one?

Next in succession was Huineng who is known as the Sixth Patriarch.[7] What is interesting about him is he had no formal education and no training as a Buddhist monk or priest. He is said to have attained awakening on reading the Diamond Sutra. His story is interesting since there was a well-known teacher, Yuquin Shenxiu, who had already been announced as the successor. But the untrained, uneducated Huineng was chosen instead. Apparently, part of the decision was a poetry competition. Shenxiu's submission was:

> *The body is the bodhi tree.*
> *The mind is like a bright mirror's stand.*
> *At all times we must strive to polish it*
> *and must not let dust collect.*

The outgoing patriarch was unimpressed, and found Huineng's offering far more appealing:

> *The bright mirror is*
> *originally clear and pure.*
> *Where could there be any dust?*

Perhaps not surprisingly given the nature of his awakening experience, the Sixth Patriarch is known as the founder of the "Sudden Enlightenment" Southern Chan School of Buddhism. One of his students wrote down his teachings and that text is known as the *Platform Sutra of the Sixth Patriarch*. It is a central text in East Asian Buddhism. Whereas the Southern School espoused this idea of sudden awakening, the Northern School headed up by Shenxiu proclaimed that awakening is gradual. Eventually the southern school dissolved into various new schools, and the northern school faded out. But the difference of opinion between Zen (Chan) masters between sudden awakening and gradual awakening has continued—you will find those who continue to argue this issue today.

In the ensuing age of Chan, the Caodong school (which became the Soto school in Japan) espoused "silent illumination" arising from persistent wall-gazing. Whereas those coming from the rival Linji (Rinzai in Japan) school spoke out loudly against such an idea. Dahui Zonggao, a leading teacher in the Linji tradition, was particularly vocal in his criticism of silent illumination—or *shikantaza* as the Caogdong (Soto) school called it—and instead promoted gong-an (koan) practice. He introduced *kan huatou* ("inspecting the critical or head phrase") which became known as koan introspection and word head practice *hua tou* (*hwadu*, Kr; *wato*, Jp). He is quoted as referring to the *"heretical Chan of silent illumination"* of the Caodong (Soto) school.

There is growing acceptance, though, that awakening is neither just sudden (*satori*) nor is it solely gradual leading to a one-time awakening or *satori*. Instead, for most people awakening is a series of awakening moments (Soto calls them *kensho*—a glimpse into one's true nature) interspersed by gradual cultivation of the experience and further realization. Buddha taught for more than 40 years after his experience under the Bodhi tree, and it appears he continued to refine his awakening over the balance of his life.

After Huineng, from around 710 C.E., Chan Buddhism split into five different branches known as The Five Houses: the Guiyang school, the Linji school, the Caodong school, the Fayan school and the Yunmen school. The first breakaway sect to emerge was the Guiyang school which is often described as being associated with the use of mystical symbols. In fact, may practices this school introduced form common, even iconic, elements of modern Zen.

For instance, they introduced the use of a circle as a key symbol in Chan, and the use of symbolic action rather than words as part of teaching. While the iconic *enso* may be thought of as quintessentially Japanese, it could date back to this school's use of circles. Similarly, the fact it is common in koan introspection to seek an action in response rather than words may have roots in this school's practices.

Qingyuan Xingsi and Shitou Xiqian (Shih-t'ou Hsi-ch'ien; 700-790 C.E.) were two other major figures in this early evolution of Zen. Of the five schools of Zen that flowered at this time, three of them are connected to them: the Fayan, Yunmen and Caodong schools. Shitou was just thirteen when the Huineng died. Legend says that when the sixth ancestor was on his deathbed, he whispered to Shitou "Go to Qingyuan Xingsi" who was one of Huineng's head monks.

But Shitou apparently heard "hsun szu" which means to meditate, since it sounds similar in Chinese. As the story goes, he then meditated for an extended period until someone realized his error and connected him with Xingsi. He eventually founded his own teaching center and taught there for 25 years.

Nanyue Huariang (677-744) was the premiere student of the sixth ancestor and headed up the school that developed into the main form of Chan in China, the Linji school. His most notable student was Mazu Daoyi (709-788) who became a key figure in the development of Chinese Chan in this period. Mazu's teaching style and what he taught are legendary in Zen circles because he became a key part of the break from mainstream Chan focus on meditation. Mazu became famous in the monastery for extended wall-gazing sessions, so one day his master came to him and asked why did he sit for so long gazing at walls? This is what is recorded happened next:

Mazu: "I want to become a Buddha, an enlightened being."

Saying nothing, the master quietly picked up a brick and started rubbing it on a stone.

Curious after watching the master for a while, Mazu: "Why are you rubbing that brick on a stone?"

Huairang: "I am polishing it into a mirror."

Mazu probably knew by this time that he had been set up, but he had to follow through: "But how can you make a mirror by polishing a brick on a stone?"

The master: "How can you become enlightened by sitting in meditation?"

Arising from the teachings he received from Huairang, Mazu went on to teach those who in turn taught Linji, after whom the leading school of Chinese Chan was named. Core to this approach to Zen is the idea that awakening isn't something you "attain" through some artificial passive practice, but it is arrived at by being active and integrating Zen practice into everyday life. Nanquan Puyuan was a dharma successor of Mazu, and he and his student, Zhaozhou Congshen, became well-known for their appearances in various Zen koans. Nanquan appears as a competent student on various koans, and later appears as a master teaching others. He is mentioned in four koans in *The Gateless Gate* book of koans, six in *The Blue Cliff Record*, and three in *The Book of Equanimity*.

Perhaps one of the best known koans featuring Nanquan also features Zhaozhou (Joshu, Jp) as the student:

> One day at Nanquan's the eastern and western halls were
>   arguing over a cat. When Nanquan saw this, he took and
>   held it up and said, "If you can speak I won't cut it."
> The group had no reply;
> Nanquan then cut the cat in two.
> Nanquan also brought up the foregoing incident to
>   Zhaozhou and asked him:
> Zhaozhou immediately took off his sandals, put them on his
>   head, and left.
> Nanquan said, "If you had been here you could have saved
>   the cat."

Nanquan was well known for rather theatrical teachings, here is another:

> Lu Hsuan: "What if I told you that a man had raised a
>   goose in a bottle, watching it grow until one day he
>   realized that it had grown too large to pass through the
>   bottle's neck? Since he did not want to break the bottle or
>   kill the goose, how would he get it out?"
> Nanquan (beginning quietly): "My esteemed governor . . . "
> Then shouting: ". . . THE GOOSE IS OUT!"

And another:

A monk to Nanquan: "There is a jewel in the sky; how can we
get hold of it?"
Nanquan: "Cut down bamboos and make a ladder, put it up
in the sky, and get hold of it!"
The monk: "How can the ladder be put up in the sky?"
Nanquan: "How can you doubt your getting hold of the
jewel?""

Common to the teaching style introduced by Nanquan is both that it involves koans rather than a focus on wall-gazing, and that he emphasized the use of responding in such a way as to indicate awareness of being stuck in a net of words, where a *non sequitur* response can reveal the student is free of the net—that said, what many believe are *non sequiturs* are often a failure of the person to appreciate the teaching. As koans later became more formalized by the likes of Dahui (1089-1163), his approach to koan teaching would become one of several recognized kinds of koan. By the way, it is very unlikely that Nanquan actually hurt a cat.

The year 845 C.E. brought the Great Buddhist Persecution in China, executed by the Tang Emperor Wuzong. The idea was to cleanse China of foreign influence, which the emperor saw Indian-based Buddhism as being. Although the persecution only lasted just under two years, it devastated Chinese Buddhism in general including the still newly evolving Chan schools.

When the dust settled around 847 C.E. three of the Chan schools were essentially gone, leaving the two main schools of Linji and Caodong, which went on to form the cornerstone of

Zen both in Asia and the West. The Linji school emerged the strongest of the Chan schools, and remains the strongest in China to this day. A close second was the Caodong school, and of course these two were later exported to Japan as the Rinzai and Soto schools there.

The Linji school took its name from the Chan master Linji Yixuan (died 866 C.E.). He is known for being rough with his students, shouting at them and hitting them in order to provoke sudden awakening. The story of his own awakening reflects his later teaching style. He was based at Huangbo's monastery and practiced hard for three years. In his encounter with Huangbo he was asked *"What is the meaning of Bodhidharma's coming from the West?"* When he failed to respond, Huangbo hit him hard with his stick. Every time he returned, he faced the same aggressive response from his teacher.

In frustration at seeming to get nowhere with his practice at the monastery he announced he was leaving to pursue his training elsewhere. Linji was surprised that Huangbo seemed very understanding of his desire to try elsewhere and directed him to a much gentler teacher at a nearby monastery, master Dayu. Once there Linji complained bitterly to Dayu about how badly he had been treated by Huangbo. In response Dayu told him that Huangbo had treated him with great compassion and just wanted to relieve Linji's distress.

With this we are told in *The Record of the Lamp* Linji had a sudden awakening and realized the wordless insight Huangbo was trying to transmit to him. He returned to study with Huangbo as one of the master's leading students. From this arose the Linji school, with a focus on sudden awakening occurring after a substantial period of disciplined preparation.

The other main surviving Chan sect was the Coadong school, named after a key student of Shitou, Dongshan, and Dongshan's pupil Caoshan. This school thus takes its name from parts of these two teacher's names. Dongshan Liangjie started his training in a very strict rule-based vinaya[8] sect where he got a reputation for asking probing questions. After a session in which he was challenging his superiors on their understanding of the Heart Sutra, he was advised to leave and join a Chan school. He dutifully left to join Nanquan's monastery where he impressed Nanquan with the depth of his appreciation of the dharma.

By 860 C.E. Dongshan had his own monastery and many followers who wanted to study with him. Whereas the Linji teachers had become known for speaking what others saw as absurdities, Dongshan preferred to speak in metaphor. Here is an example of an exchange between him and one of his monks:

> A monk asked, "When the cold season comes, where can one go to avoid it?"
> Dongshan said, "Why not go where there is no cold?"
> The monk said, "What is the place where there's no cold?"
> Dongshan said, "When it's cold, the cold kills you. When it's hot, the heat kills you."

And another exchange:

> Dongshan asked a monk, "Where have you been?"
> The monk said, "Walking on the mountain."
> Dongshan said, "Did you reach the peak?'

The monk said, "I reached it."

Dongshan said, "Were there people there?"

The monk said, "There weren't any people."

Dongshan said, "In that case you didn't reach the peak."

*The monk said, "If I haven't been to the peak, how would I
know there are no people?"*

Dongshan said, "Why didn't you stay there?"

*The monk said, "I would stay there, but there's someone in
India who would disapprove."*

Dongshan said, "Formerly I doubted this fellow."

Dongshan's most successful student was Coashan Benji. Dongshan had developed what he called the "Five Ranks" as core to the method of teaching Zen, and Coashan built upon this technique to form the Caodong school that was eventually introduced by Dogen Zenji to Japan as the Soto school. The Five Ranks are:

1. *The Relative within the Absolute*
2. *The Absolute within the Relative*
3. *Coming from within the Absolute*
4. *Arrival at Mutual Integration*
5. *Unity Attained.*

The ranks, then, act as a series of guideposts on the road to awakening, echoing the Coadong preference for silent illumination, slow gradual steps with a focus on meditation. Interestingly, the five ranks make a reappearance of sorts in the teachings of Seung Sahn, the 20th century Korean Zen Master teaching within the Linji school and are reflected in his book *The Compass of Zen*.

During the period 900 to 1200 C.E. the Linji school rose to prominence in China, and with it came a formalization of the practice of koan introspection. The earliest record we have of encounter dialogues is the *Anthology of the Ancestral Hall* compiled around the year 952 C.E. By the way, you will often find this text referred to as the *Anthology of the Patriarchal Hall* but Chinese is not gendered, and the Chinese characters in question are usually translated as "ancestral."

This work dates from around 500 years before the better-known work *The Jingde Record of the Transmission of the Lamp*. It was only relatively recently discovered in the 20th century by researchers working at the Haeinsa temple in Korea. Until the discovery of this text, the *Transmission of the Lamp* dating from around 1004-1007 C.E. was thought to be the earliest record of koan stories. The other three early Chan collections of koans were *The Blue Cliff Record*, *The Book of Equanimity* and *The Gateless Gate* (*Mumonkan*, Jp).

The Bluecliff Record is a collection of one hundred koans collected by the Chan master Xuetou Chongxian (980-1052) who attached a small poem to each koan. Later, a Linji master Yuanwu Keqin (1063-1135) embellished the original to the form it is generally known now. He added extensive commentaries on each koan, which some later authors would omit, adding their own commentaries instead. This collection of koans became central to the Linji (Rinzai) tradition and remains an important source book of koans to this day.

The *Wumenguan* (*Mumonkan*, Jp), also known as *The Gateless Gate*, is the other key Linji (Rinzai) collection of koans. It is a collection of 48 koans compiled by the Chan master Wumen Huikai (1183-1260). Since the Chan master's name literally means "no gate" or "no barrier," the title of the work can be read two ways as either the Wumen's Gate or the Gateless Gate. In the introduction to the work it states that it was compiled in the year 1228. This work, and the *Blue Cliff Record*, are the core source of koans in the Linji (Rinzai) tradition.

A third collection of koans from this early era is *The Book of Equanimity*, also known as the *Book of Serenity*, which is a collection of one hundred koans similar to the *Blue Cliff*, but this time collected by the Caodong (Soto) Chan master Hongzhi Zhengjue (1091-1157).

A review of this early formation of Chan Buddhism would not be complete without mention of the Linji Chan master, Dahui Zonggao (1089-1163). Dahui was the premiere Chan master during the Song dynasty and is responsible for the first real organization of koan teaching in the Linji tradition. He also introduced the idea of *kan huatou* (hwadu, Kr; wato, Jp) practice. This practice grew out of the basic koan introspection practice and focuses on just the "word head" or "head of speech" of a koan, which is what the term means.

Dahui reacted against the intellectualization of koan practice by his time, and even burnt all the copies of *The Blue Cliff Record* he could find and burnt to wooden printing blocks for it, too (later, his students found a few copies and made new wooden tablets to print it again). He sought to replace koan practice with a focus on these word-head phrases, such as working with the phrase "Who am I?" or "What is this?" or "Who is dragging this corpse around?" The practice emphasizes continual practice, all day each day, rather than a practice limited to a room where one meditates facing a wall, or a brief interaction with a teacher working on a given koan.

Dahui was a fierce critic of the Caodong (Soto) school's emphasis on just sitting (*shikantaza*, Jp) also known as *silent illumination*. He referred to such practices as heretical Chan. His main written work was a collection of koans named *Zhengfa Yanzang* (*The Treasury of the True Dharma Eye*). The Japanese monk who later brought Soto Zen to Japan, Dogen, was to later use the exact same name for his best-known work, which is somewhat ironic given Dogen is often seen as the leading proponent of the practice Dahui was most critical of—just sitting, or *shikantaza*.

In this same timeframe—900-1200 C.E.—Chan Buddhism spread first to Korea (as Seon) and then to Japan (as Zen). In fact, there is some evidence that Seon Buddhism was first brought to Korea in the early 7th century by Beomnang who studied with the fourth ancestor Daoxin in China before bringing the teachings back to Korea. Seon was then further expanded by Korean master teacher Doui is the 9th century and he is recognized as the first patriarch of Korean Seon.

This led to the formation of what became known as the "Nine Mountain Schools" in the 800-900 period, with the first formal record of the nine schools dating from 1084. The nine schools were: The *Ganji San* school founded by Borimsa (804-890); The S*eongju* school founded by Muyeom (800-888); The *Silisangsan* school founded by Hongcheok (~830); The *Huiyang san* school founded by Beomnang and Chiseon Doheon (824-882); The *Bongnim san* school founded by Weongam (787-869); The *Dongni san* school founded by Hyejeol (785-861); The *Sangul san* school founded by Beom'il (810-889); The *Saja san* school founded by Doyun (797-868) and The *Sumi san* school founded by Ieom (869-936).

The first 8 were derived from Chan Linji schools, and the ninth emerged from the Caodong lineage. Unlike the strict division of schools (for instance Soto and Rinzai in Japan), in Korea it would not be unusual for a campus to have a mix of different Seon schools represented with students being encouraged to move from school to school as part of their practice.

Linji Chan Buddhism was established in Japan as Rinzai Buddhism in 1168, having been introduced there by the monk Myoan Eisai. In the 18th century the Rinzai tradition in Japan was revitalized by the Zen Master Hakuin Ekaku. In the earlier period the koan Mu (Wu in Chinese) had become a central koan for those engaged in koan introspection. But by the time of Hakuin the koan work had become highly formalized and intellectualized: students would carry small books stuffed into their robes containing the phrases they should say to their teacher during a fact to face interview (*dokusan*, Jp). Hakuin thus decided to retire the koan Mu as the primary one used and invented his own introductory koan.

This koan went on to become—albeit in misquoted form—one of the most well-known koans in popular culture. The koan has entered the mass market as *"What is the sound of one hand clapping?"* although this is not the true koan Hakuin invented. Rather his koan notes that, *"We know the sound two hands clapping make, "What is the sound of one hand?"* To the uninitiated these may seem similar questions, but to those with a practice of koan introspection they are worlds different. Only the latter works as a koan.

The other main Chinese Chan school, Caodong, was introduced to Japan in 1227 by Dogen Zenji. Once in Japan it became known as Soto Zen Buddhism—the most widely known form of Zen in the West today. Indeed, the reason we tend to call this form of Buddhism "Zen" is due to the success of the Japanese Soto Zen school in the West.

Know your Buddhas

We all know what the Buddha looks like, right? Fat, big bellied, happy fellow? Well, no, that isn't a depiction of Gautama Buddha, that is Budai (*Hotei*, Jp), a semi-mythical 10th century Chan monk venerated as *Maitreya Buddha* (the future Buddha) in China. He found his way into the Japanese gallery of Buddhist imagery, and is known by various other names such as the Fat Buddha, or the Laughing Buddha. But he isn't the historic Buddha, Siddhartha Gautama, despite many people thinking he is.

You've probably seen the sculptures of Buddha looking like a Greek statue. Well, there is a very good reason they look like Greek statues, because they *are* Greek statues. While Buddhism is often thought of as purely Indian, a sizable influence on Buddhism worldwide is the absorption of Buddhism into Hellenistic culture by the 4th century B.C.E. Greco-Buddhism flourished until around the first century C.E. when it was absorbed into the Kushan Empire, which continued to spread the Greco-Buddhism from its cultural center in Bactria, Northern India, eastwards to China.

Not surprisingly, then, many of the statues of Buddha from this early era of the 1st and 2nd century C.E. are rendered in the same style as Greek statues of gods, emperors, and etc.

More traditional depictions of Buddha show him in a highly stylized form, indeed traditionally there are thirty-two marks that distinguish him and a further eighty secondary marks. All of the features you may have seen owe themselves to these lists of his special features: the top knot sitting on top of snail-shaped curls, the long ears, and a dot in the center of the forehead to indicate a third eye. His hands will usually be in one of several poses known as "mudras." Often the statue simply depicts Buddha in a hands one under the other meditation pose (so-called cosmic mudra) or sometimes with the left palm up and the right pointing down is the mudra of touching the earth which represents the moment of Buddha's awakening.

One further image you may come across is one of what may seem to be a female Buddha. These are depictions of the Guan Yin (or Kuan Yin), also known as *Avalokitesvara*, the Mahayana Buddhist bodhisattva of compassion.

---

[3] Liu Xinru, *The Silk Road in History*, Oxford University Press, 2010, 42.
[4] S.G. Goodrich, *A History of All Nations*, Derby & Miller, 1874.
[5] *Encyclopedia of Buddhism*, Macmillan, 2003 57, 130.

[6] This exchange is recounted in the first koan of the *Blue Cliff Record*.

[7] Chinese has no gender, so strictly speaking while many writers use the term "Patriarch" the better term would be "Ancestor."

[8] I discuss the vinaya elsewhere in this book.

To travel is to be alive, but to get somewhere is to be dead, for as our own proverb says, "To travel well is better than to arrive."

Alan Watts

four

Zen in the West

Many point to the World Parliament of Religions meeting in Chicago in 1893 as the moment Buddhism was introduced to the West. This is naïve, of course, since awareness of Buddhism in the West had been widespread for a considerable time by that point. However, present at that meeting in Chicago was the Japanese Rinzai Roshi Soyen Shaku who was Daisetsu Teitaro Suzuki's teacher. This was an auspicious event in that upon his return to Japan Roshi Soyen dispatched D.T. Suzuki (as he is usually known) to America to teach the West about Zen.

D.T. Suzuki (1870-1966) went on to write some of the first books on Zen in the English language. There is no doubt that Suzuki's books had tremendous influence on those interested in learning about Zen. Between 1927 and 1934 he published three volumes of his "*Essays in Zen Buddhism,*" followed in the next two years by "*An Introduction to Zen Buddhism,*" "*The Training of a Zen Buddhist Monk,*" and "*Manual of Zen Buddhism.*"

Among those inspired by D.T. Suzuki was the British author Alan Watts, who went on to write numerous books on Zen which many in the West credit with getting them started on the Zen path. Watts was both prolific and a prodigy. He was just seventeen when he wrote his first text on Zen in 1932, "*An Outline of Zen Buddhism.*" He went on to write his 1948 book simply titled *"Zen,"* and then in 1957 he wrote his seminal work, *"The Way of Zen."* Watts was born in Chislehurst, England, and moved to New York in 1938. He then attended Seabury-Western Theological Seminary in Illinois and was ordained an Episcopal Priest in 1945. Barely five years later, he left the church and moved to the Bay Area in California where he lived the rest of his life.

I recall in the late 1960s and very early 1970s my introduction to Zen was through books by D.T. Suzuki and Watt's *"The Way of Zen."* The Suzuki works—with introductions by the delightfully named Christmas Humphreys, President of the British Buddhist Society—were tough going for me. By contrast, Watt's writing was accessible and (by contrast) a breath of fresh air. That is not to say D.T. Suzuki's books are not excellent, they are. Nor is it to say that all of Watt's books make for easy reading, they do not.

The other two books I recall reading at the start of my Zen journey were *"The Three Pillars of Zen,"* by Philip Kapleau, and *"Zen Flesh, Zen Bones,"* by Paul Reps. To this day, these are still among the books I recommend to those interested in discovering more about Zen. The other book that I read in these early days is sadly no longer in print: *"Zen, A Way of Life"* by Christmas Humphreys. I still cherish my 1962 edition of his work and continue to be amused by the reason he states for writing the book:

> *To check, if possible, the growth in England of anything like the 'Beat Zen' of the U.S.A., where the term Zen, with little if any understanding of its meaning, has been adopted by certain lost, unhappy minds of the younger generation to express their own*

subconscious fears and longings, and to give them a
rational excuse for mental and moral misbehaviour.
(1962, 1)

Traditional academically oriented Buddhist scholars like Christmas Humphreys were horrified that the beat generation poets, with the likes of Allen Ginsberg and Gary Snyder, had appropriated Zen for their own popularist purposes. Yet despite his fear of the rise of Beat Zen in America, out of that brief movement came seeds of establishment of Zen in the States. Gary Snyder has gone on to become a highly respected environmental activist as well as a Pulitzer Award winning poet. Another "Beat," Phil Whalen, went on to become abbot of the Hartford Street Zen Center in San Francisco.

In the early 1950s, the Sanbo Kyoden School of Zen was founded in Japan by Yasutani Roshi and his student Koun Yamada. They then brought their unique blend of Zen to America, being a combination of *shikantaza* zazen meditation (Soto style) with koan introspection (Rinzai style). And from this early American school emerged such influential Zen teachers as Robert Aitken Roshi who went on to write several important works on Zen. Aitken established his "Diamond Sangha" in Honolulu in 1959, and although he received Dharma Transmission from Koun Yamada in 1985, he decided to remain a lay teacher.

Over this period of the 1950s and 1960s various Zen teachers came to America from China, Korea and Japan. A key figure among them was Taizan Maezumi Roshi who founded the Zen Center of Los Angeles (ZCLA) in 1967. Maezumi's lineage is known as the White Plum Asanga and

73

is thriving to this day with well-known Zen teachers such Bernie Glassman, Joko Beck, John Daido Loori, Jan Chozen Bays, Wendy Egyoku Nakao, and, through Glassman, Joan Halifax.

The White Plum Asanga now has several Zen centers around the U.S., including Yokoji Zen Mountain Center, Zen Mountain Monastery, Upaya Institute and Zen Center, Village Zendo, the New York Zen Center for Contemplative Care. ZCLA was the first Zen Center I visited in the early 1970s, and where I met Maezumi Roshi, and to which I returned in the mid-1990s when Bernie Glassman was heading it up, Maezumi having just passed. I later went on to study Buddhist Chaplaincy at another White Plum center, Upaya, under the leadership of Joan Halifax.

Another center I spent time at in the early 1970s was Tassajara Zen Mountain Center. Tassajara is one of the three practice places of San Francisco Zen Center, along with Beginner's Mind Temple and Green Gulch Farm. SFZC was established in 1962 by the remarkable Zen teacher, Shunryu Suzuki Roshi. His book, *Zen Mind, Beginner's Mind,"* is still a classic work highly recommended to this day. You may also find the book about Suzuki of interest, *Crooked Cucumber.* SFZC is also known for the many ventures it started, such as a bakery, a restaurant and the first American Buddhist Hospice (which sadly had to close its doors in 2018 due to lack of financial support).

Philip Kapleau is another key figure in the early introduction of Zen to the West. He trained with both Soto and Rinzai schools in Japan and studied with both Harada and Yasutani. His book, *The Three Pillars of Zen*, was one of the first that I read, and remains a key Zen introductory text to this day, if somewhat narrow in its focus.

Korean Zen was introduced in the U.S. by various Seon teachers, of which probably the best known is the Korean Seon master teacher, Seung Sahn. He was a Zen master in the Jogye Order and founded the highly successful Kwan Um School of Zen in the States. Born in 1927 in what is now North Korea, he was raised in a Presbyterian family. Accounts tell of how in was given a copy of the Diamond Sutra and this sparked his journey in Zen, with him taking the precepts in 1948.

Having served as an army chaplain in the Republic of Korea army in the early 1950s, he then went on to found Buddhist temples in Hong Kong and Japan. Starting in 1974, he began founding Zen centers across America, commencing with one in Providence, Rhode Island, and then later in New York and elsewhere.

The Kwan Um school itself formally came into being in 1983, and its set itself apart from other Zen centers by actively encouraging lay practitioners to wear robes. He gave transmission to various people who then, directly and through subsequent transmissions, went on to found Zen centers outside of the core Kwan Um school. Such centers include Golden Wind Zen Center founded by Venerable Wonji Dharma as Abbot, and run by Master Ji Bong, and Five Mountain Zen Order (FMZO), established by Wonji Dharma.

FMZO is also in the Vietnamese Zen (Thien) lineage of Thich Thien-An, who is one of the other Zen masters to bring Zen to the West. Thien-An came to the United States in 1966 and taught philosophy at the University of California, Los Angeles. He started some casual Zen sitting groups, and his students encouraged him to establish a more formal Zen center. This resulted in him founding the *International Buddhist Meditation Center* in Los Angeles in 1970.

As Zen spread to the West, it did not do so in the form that it was being practiced in China, Japan, Korea or Vietnam. As was appropriate, Zen was immediately reshaped and remodeled to fit western culture. This is not to say that you cannot get an "authentic" Japanese Zen experience in America: for instance, the Japanese Sotoshu have centers in the U.S. that are run more closely to how they are run in Japan. Even then, they make significant accommodations for having an American, rather than Japanese, audience.

The Soto Zen Buddhism center in the U.S. was established in 1937, based at the Zenshuji Soto Mission in Los Angeles. The connection was established with the Japanese head temples of Eiheiji (founded by Dogen) and Sojiji, and that connection remains to this day. But a visit to a Southern California Soto location—such as Zenshuji in Los Angeles, Sozenji in Montebello, or the Long Beach Buddhist Church—will likely not be what you expect.

The spaces are set up like a Western Christian church with many rows of pews. Up on a stage at the front of the church is the area that the Zen monks and priest perform their liturgy, as a performance the attendees are witnessing, rather than participating in. The practice is stricter than in most American (or European) Zen centers, with a lot of precision to the liturgy and the careful choreography of movement and chanting. Some have commented that it is "too Japanese" for American tastes. Others are grateful the more authentic Japanese practice is available in the U.S.

Having undergone Soto priest training at two of these locations, I understand the sentiments. Indeed, it will be a challenge for Sotoshu in the U.S. to decide how they can change to better attract American students, or indeed whether they should make such changes or remain faithful to the Soto traditions of the home centers in Japan.

Zen in the West is young—at the time of writing it is barely more than 50 years since the initial establishment of Zen centers here. Zen in the Americas, and in Europe, then, is still in its nascent phase, still growing and adapting to western culture. In Japan, for instance, a young man in a family might have been compelled—or at least be strongly pressured—to join a Zen monastery in order to continue a family tradition of running the center. A sizable part of the motivation may have been financial, since without such familial support with each new generation the centers would not survive.

Similarly, in Japan it has tended to be a male oriented culture, where nuns have a place, but it can tend to be a lesser place in the hierarchy. The idea of becoming a monk and living in a Zen monastery is more the norm, whereas here in the West monks and nuns living in a Zen center is the exception not the norm. Similarly, American Zen flourished in part because it has both women and men leading various groups and centers.

Zen in America has been accompanied by a rise of lay practitioner Zen: while some may follow a path that leads to ordination as either a monk or priest, the majority of Zen students simply attend centers to sit zazen or, to a lesser extent, participate in koan introspection. Similarly, lay practitioners take the precepts which leads to them wearing a rakusu (Japanese tradition) or a wagasa (Korean), and priests and monks wearing robes and kesas (Japanese) or robes and bangasa (Korean). Many of such monks and priests being treated in their traditions as lay, rather than formally ordained as they would be in the East. That said, the idea of "lay ordination" (which sounds like an oxymoron to anyone coming from a Western religious perspective) appears to be more common in Japanese based American Soto centers as they seek to accommodate what they see as local cultural demands.

Zen Ranks and Titles

The various titles and ranks of Zen in the West can be confusing. For instance, the term "roshi" has come to mean "Zen master" for many in the West, whereas the term in Japan simply means "old master" and could be used by any elder teacher over 60 years of age. Here in the West it now tends to be reserved for those who have received full transmission (or *inka shomei*); in the Rinzai tradition it may mean the person completed the entire koan curriculum, in the Soto tradition it may simply mean their teacher believes they are worthy of the full transmission.

In America and Europe almost any teacher who has received dharma transmission might call themselves a roshi, whereas that would not happen in Japan. In Japan there is an emphasis on dharma transmission, but it is most usually associated with determining who will own and run a temple. In Soto there are four dharma ranks (*hokai*) and eight priest ranks (*sokai*). In training the student takes *shukke tokudo* to become a priest. As a novice priest the student will have a shaved head and permission to wear priest robes. From here one becomes an *Unsui*, a training monk, where they attain the rank of *joza*.

When they have been training for at least three years, the rank of *risshin* is attainable and they will take part in a *hossen-shiki* ceremony (known as dharma combat) while working as *shuso* or head monk. Dharma combat in the Japanese tradition has some similarity to its Western counterpart: in both instances the candidate is asked questions and they must answer them satisfactorily.

In Japan these can be a very scripted event, where the candidate has memorized exactly what to say. Here in the West, Soto centers have tended to have teachers and members of a dharma combat audience ask questions without a script. That said, I have never heard of any candidate "losing" the combat, it is seen more as a ceremonial affirmation rather than an actual test.

The third step is *shiho* or denpo, dharma transmission. In traditional Soto circles, this happens only once and permanently binds a student to a particular teacher. To become an *Osho*, or full teacher, further steps are needed. When completed the student may then progress from wearing the traditional black robes and kesa, to black robes with an ochre colored kesa.

Sanbo Kyodan by contrast is a lay lineage that combines elements of both the Soto and Rinzai schools. There are two levels of teach authority, *Junshike* ("associate Zen master") and *shoshike* ("authentic or full Zen master"). When the student receives dharma transmission they get the *sanmotsu*, which is a lay form of the Soto *shiho* ceremony. If a student completes the entire koan curriculum they may then receive what is termed *inka*.

The Kwan Um school established by Seung Sahn devised its own unique levels of being a teacher. A basic dharma teacher is someone who has taken the five and ten precepts and a minimum of four years training. A senior dharma teacher (SDPS) needs at least five years training after becoming a Dharma Teacher and takes the sixteen precepts. They can work with students unsupervised but cannot work on kong'ans with students. A Ji Do Poep Sa Nim (JDPSN) is a teacher who has completed the koan (kong-an) training and receives *inka*. At this level the teacher can teach on their own without supervision. Finally, there is the step of Soen Sa Nim which is this school's equivalent of "Zen master" or roshi and is a final transmission from one master to another.

Addiction Issues and Misconduct Allegations

Unfortunately, Buddhism in the West has been plagued by serious issues with its leading figures, including sexual misconduct and alcoholism. Alan Watts, for instance died at just 58 years old due to medical issues arising from his chronic alcoholism. Similarly, Maezumi Roshi died at just 64 years old as a result of his alcoholism. On a trip back to Japan, he consumed too much alcohol, fell asleep in his hot tub and drowned.

Wendy Egyoku Nakao Roshi, who became abbot of the Zen Center of Los Angeles after Maezumi died, spoke of running the center as feeling like "just sitting within the burned out field" because so many students left as a result of his alcoholism and sexual relationships with students.

In 2014, Zen master Joshu Sasaki Roshi of the Runzai-ji Zen Center in Los Angeles was accused of abusing hundreds of students over decades. Another example of this shameful trend was Eido Shimano who ran a Zen center in New York, and who received the title "The Zen Predator of the Upper East Side."[1] Shimano's bad behavior with women was known about for years, but the sangha enabled it to continue far beyond the point it should have been halted.

Sadly, these are not the only examples of sexual misconduct accusations in Western Buddhism, or examples of leading figures falling foul to alcohol or other addictions. In 2019, two more leading figures either stepped back from teaching (Shambala head Sakyong Mipham Rinpoche) or had their authority revoked (Noah Levine; Spirit Rock Meditation Center and the Against the Stream Meditation Society).

At the time of writing, the Western Zen Buddhist world has had a year with few if any further instances of such behavior[2] and one can only hope that this remains the case going forward. But this sheds a spotlight on one aspect of Zen in the West, namely that while many Eastern Buddhist monastic sects were founded to closely follow strict behavior and moral guidelines (known as the Vinaya), Japanese Zen does not tend to recognize such ethical and moral guidelines. And, in turn, Western Zen was seeded in large part by the Japanese schools.

As a consequence, there has perhaps been a historical lack of needed emphasis on ethical and moral behavior in Western Zen centers, but the hope is that this is changing at this time. The other issue this threw light on was Zen center leaders who were unprepared for the power their position held, and thus abused that power. Whatever the reason, one can only hope that Zen in the West has turned a corner on such issues and will in future be known for adhering to high ethical and moral standards.

There is one further issue this has thrown light on, too, namely that becoming "enlightened" (awakened) is no guarantee that life will be easy and filled with nothing but happiness. Rather, having an awakening experience (*kensho* in the Japanese tradition) can potentially lead to depression and despondency if the student's progress is not carefully curated by working closely with a mentor or teacher. There can be a trap that some students of the Zen way fall into of waking up one day and saying to themselves, "*Is this all there is to it?*" Or a more subtle form of dissatisfaction with life, despite (or maybe because of) great progress in Zen practice, that in turn leads to substance abuse or addiction.

In other non-dual, mystical or monastic traditions, such as those associated with Christianity, the "*dark night of the soul*" is a known phenomenon. Practicing Zen is no different, it too can have its own periods of a "dark night" and it is a matter of knowing when to turn to another for help if that happens. It also underscores the need for all serious followers of the Zen way to find themselves a mentor or teacher that they meet with (in person or virtually) on a regular basis.

Syncretic Zen

I mentioned at the outset of this book that Zen seems to have entered almost every corner of Western society: wherever there is something that is minimalist, or which promotes relaxation, Zen gets added to the name: Zen Spas, Zen interior design, Zen relaxing bubble bath.

But there are other ways in which Zen has integrated to some degree or other with Western culture and established religion. Zen has the advantage that since it is a way of life, or a "spiritual practice," it can coexist alongside other religions or religious practices. This has been the case for those who have become distance from the faith of their birth or upbringing and found a new home in Zen. For instance, so popular is Zen with people of Jewish background that the term "Jewbu" was coined. Notable Jewbus include Leonard Cohen, Robert Downey Jr., Allen Ginsberg, Phillip Glass, Bernie Glassman, Natalie Goldberg, Goldie Hawn, Jon Kabat-Zinn, Jack Kornfield, Mandy Patinkin, Jeremy Piven, and Sharon Salzberg. And there are of course numerous Christians, Muslims, Hindus and those from virtually all worldwide faiths and spiritual paths who also practice Zen.

Zen has also become part of more commonplace Christianity in the form of Centering prayer (which is based on Zen meditation) and now Kenosis or Kenotic Meditation with my books on that topic of a deeper Christian mediation practice derived from Zen practices. Buddhist meditation has also become popular simply by being known as "mindfulness," as in the Mindfulness Based Stress Reduction program devised by Jon Kabat-Zinn. Although strict practitioners of zazen tend to distance themselves from popularized mindfulness programs and practices, as being not authentic Buddhism or authentic Zen.

---

[1] Mark Oppenheimer, *The Zen Predator of the Upper East Side*, The Atlantic, December 18, 2014.

[2] Sadly, while editing this book another example is just being reported: allegations of sexual misconduct by Lama Surya Das.

Zen pretty much comes down to three things— everything changes; everything is connected; pay attention.

Jane Hirshfield

five

Zen Principles

The main principles of Buddhism can be summarized as The Three Signs of Being, The Four Nobel Truths, including the Middle Way of the Nobel Eightfold Path, Karma and rebirth, Concentration and Meditation, the focus on tolerance and the place of Nirvana in the teachings.

The Three Signs of Being

In Buddhism the characteristics of existence are not doctrine but are fact that each student should test before accepting them. The way the Buddha described it is, all aggregates, compounded things, compounds or formations, are *anicca* and subject to change. They are also *dukkha*, which means they are inseparable from suffering. And lastly, they are all found to be *anatta*, which means they are devoid of a separate self or identity.

In his first discourse at the Deer Park, Buddha introduced his Four Noble Truths:
- Suffering
- The cause of suffering,
- The cessation of suffering,
- The path that leads to the cessation of suffering.

The first truth of course is *dukkha*—suffering—but it has a far wider range of meaning that we usually understand by that word. Essentially, it covers all dissatisfaction about events and things, the suffering that arises when things are not as you want them to be or believe they should be. Basic suffering is included in this term, of course, but as we say, "Pain is obligatory, suffering is optional." By which we mean that following the Zen way will not mean you'll end up pain free for the rest of your life; rather it is about how you respond to pain, frustration, disappointment, and so on. The suffering—your response to stimuli—is optional, the stimuli are not.

Ultimately, then, what we mean by suffering here is anything that stands between you and accepting this moment exactly as it is. Right here, right now. So, this all goes to the second noble truth, the cause of suffering. To find the true source of suffering you need to look inside yourself and seek what you find to be the true source of your dissatisfaction, what it is that prevents you accepting the moment as it is.

The Third noble truth is basically a declaration by the Buddha that cessation of suffering is possible. And here he was not talking about taking a brief holiday from feeling down, or feeling unsatisfied with life, but a permanent cessation of suffering. This truth is essentially a request by Buddha to take on trust, as an act of faith, that suffering is optional, and it can be completely removed.

The fourth noble truth is the path to relief from suffering, which in turn is called the "Eightfold Path." The eight parts of the path are:

- Correct view—*cultivating insightful wisdom is a key first step, acquiring a clear view.*

- Correct intention—*this is the calling to right thought, to giving up selfish aims and goals, and cultivate the intention to bring cessation of suffering to all.*
- Correct speech—*the cultivation of speaking truth, speaking with kindness, and speaking what is beneficial to others.*
- Correct action—*this is the doing of no harm (ahimsa), seek to protect others, do not harm them with your actions.*
- Correct livelihood—*how you live your life, with a view to being of use to others, living with honesty and kindness.*
- Correct effort—*your spiritual practices, learning how to exert "effortless effort," and being aware of what is arising in your mind moment after moment after moment.*
- Correct mindfulness—*paying very close attention to what is happening, right here, right now.*
- Correct concentration—*the Pali word is* samadhi *and about this John Daido Loori wrote, "Samadhi is a state of consciousness that lies beyond waking, dreaming, or deep sleep. It's a slowing down of our mental activity through single-pointed concentration."* [1]

The Four Dhyanas and the Five Hindrances

The four Dhyana's (Sanskrit; also known as Jhanas in Pali) are the way to realize wisdom in the Buddha's teachings, and especially through right concentration. The goal is to be free of the delusion of a separate self, and what prevents us from doing so are the five hindrances: sensual desire, torpor, worry, ill will, and doubt. In the first Dhyana you will feel a deep sense of well-being. In the second, your monkey-mind and restless intellect recede leaving you feeling more tranquil. In the third, the feeling of well-being or rapture initially experienced recedes and is replaced by equanimity and clarity of perception. In the last, the fourth, Dhyana sensation itself ceases and only mindful equanimity remains. This final Dhyana is seen as the ultimate and is attained when the self (with a small 's') has been realized as an illusion.

Some years ago, I wrote an article I provisionally titled "The Problem of Samadhi." As of the writing of this book, the article is yet to be published but perhaps it will soon. The above four Dhyanas can be thought of as stages in Buddhist meditation, and may be more associated with Theravada practice than Mahayana. But you will come across references to samadhi in your exploration of Zen. For instance, if you attend an extended meditation retreat at a Zen center (often called a *sesshin*), you may encounter people warning you "not to break samadhi of your fellow attendees by speaking or making eye contact between sitting sessions."

What they are usually referring to is the "high" or pleasant light-headed sensation that can arise after sitting zazen for an extended period. It's possible that some believe it to be the fourth level of meditation described in the Dhyanas, but almost without exception it is an illusion, a distraction, and something so fleeting that it can be dispelled simply by making eye contact with someone else. Yet this sensation—the one you can get from extended sitting sessions—can be very seductive. I would just urge caution in not succumbing to it as some kind of "goal" in Zen. It is not.

The Three Poisons

The three poisons are: *Raga* (greed), *Dvesha* (hatred) and *Moha* (delusion). And their opposites are the three wholesome qualities: *amoha* (non-delusion) or *prajna* (wisdom); *alobha* (non-attachment) or *dana* (generosity); and *advesa* (non-hatred) or *metta* (loving-kindness). The poisons are said to drive our suffering and, predictably, the three wholesome qualities are our salvation from suffering.

These poisons underscore how unchecked thoughts and emotions can be if they are not fully understood and transformed. They can be insidious, being subtly embedded in our very conditioning and image of ourselves as separate beings—our "personalities." It may seem extreme, but the Buddha saw these poisons as the root of all suffering, yet only by taking inventory, being fully honest and transparent with ourselves can be first acknowledge them, then process them, then transform them.

The Five Skandhas

These are made of five aggregates, also termed heaps, known in Sanskrit as skandhas. They are: Form (*Rupa*), Feeling (*Vedana*), Perception (*Samjna* or *Sanna*), Mental Formations (*Samskara* or *Sankhara*), and Consciousness (*Vignana* or *Vinnana*). The last skandha is essentially the awareness of the former four. As with all conditioned phenomena, the five skandhas are subject to change and decay. Freedom from suffering comes from the realization of this and coming to peace with it. Buddha taught the skandhas are *dukka* and they are not you. They are temporary and just illusion.

The Three Treasures

The Three Treasures are the Buddha, the Dharma, and the Sangha. You will find these referred to over and again in Zen center life and practice, and for very good reason. The part of Zen liturgy where we acknowledge that we take refuge in these three treasures is similar in a way to Christians or Catholics taking holy communion. It is about as religious as Zen gets.

The Buddha

Obviously, the first treasure, the Buddha, refers to the historical figure of Shakyamuni, "the Awakened One," Siddhartha Gautama. But it also refers to the entire pantheon of Buddhas you may hear recited in a Zen center, covering all the figures who are thought to have come before Siddhartha Gautama, and all the succession of persons in a given lineage. Naturally, that will include Bodhidharma on down through the ancestors of a particular lineage, be that Korean, Vietnamese or Japanese. But its even wider than that, it also includes all bodhisattvas and mahasattvas (great beings, great bodhisattvas) throughout space and time (that is a phrase you will also hear in Zen center liturgy)—that is, all great practitioners who have realized their true self and contributed to the cessation of suffering of others.

And then there's the further twist: we are taught in Zen that we are all Buddhas. Some teachers may phrase it differently by saying we all have inherent Buddha-nature which can be realized, but it amounts to the same thing: the first treasure also encompasses us all, too. Yet of course to go around announcing you are the Buddha is a kind of delusion, too. It is not the ego centric "you" that is Buddha, rather it is the exceptionally ordinary you which in fact is the true you, and for this reason you will hear Zen teachers talking of "*Ordinary mind is the way.*"

So, this first treasure is both the Buddha and the realization (or the potential for the realization) that one is the Buddha. But it takes a tremendous amount of work to realize this.

The Dharma

The second treasure is the Dharma, and quite simply it means "truth." But you will come across it used in a variety of other ways. The mistake is to think of this treasure as just being about Buddha's teachings and the sutras, or other Buddhist texts. Yes, it is the words you read in a Buddhist text, and it's the words expounded by your teacher at the Zen center, but its also the breeze passing through the trees, the pebble held in your hand, the scientist explaining his theory, the novelist spinning a story, the blues guitarist playing her soaring solo. We talk about dharma gates being numberless, and we vow in Zen to enter them all.

Dharma literally translated means something like "cosmic law and order," but that definition can be confusing. In Zen, the meaning is often narrowed to mean the Buddha's teachings and those of notable Zen masters. We talk of "dharma transmission" which reflects the recipient having been affirmed as achieving full and complete understand of the teachings. But Mahayana texts clearly refer to something more at times with their use of the term, something closer to "manifestation of reality." The Heart Sutra for instance declares, *"Oh, Shariputra, all dharmas are marked by emptiness; they neither arise nor cease, are neither defiled nor pure, neither increase nor decrease."*

The interpenetration of everything, and the connection of everything, means that everything that happens, everything you say, do, or think, has reverberations everywhere. What we know about these reverberations is that they lead to change, simply because it is central to the teachings that there is always change. This action of the Dharma is called *karma*, perhaps one of the most misunderstood terms in Buddhism.

Karma simply means "cause and effect" but like Dharma you will come across it used in a variety of ways. Often, karma is misunderstood as simply the consequence of doing good or bad actions. Whatever you did in the past will come back to either haunt you are reward you in the future. But this is a naïve and delusional perception of reality, as if we were this powerful entity, separate from all else, causing events and experiencing the results of those specific events. The infinite sentient beings, and numberless interactions between them, means any view based solely on what "you" have said or done is at best an illusion.

Whereas in Buddhism there can be a goal of becoming free from karma, to become enlightened and get off the wheel of life and death, in Zen we discourage saying that an awakened person is either free from or subject to karma, the key is not to be reactive to it, to free oneself from blind response to it. The "Gatha of Purification" speaks to this:

All the evil karma ever created by me since of old,
on account of my beginningless greed, hatred and
   ignorance,
born of my conduct, speech, and thought,
I now fully confess it and atone for it all.

This gatha (verse) can be a major stumbling block for some starting on the Zen way. "What do you mean, on account of my *beginningless* greed, hatred and ignorance? I've only been around so many years, how can I be confessing and atoning for something *beginningless*?" But when reading Zen texts, always be on the look out for some key words like "me," "I," "mine," "myself" and so on. Here the hook word is "me," what does this mean? This goes to the core question in Zen, it is even an often used *hua tou* (*hwadu*, Kr, *wato*, Jp), "Who am I?"

Alan Watts says the following about karma which is often associated with "conditioned action:"

"Conditioned action, [is] action arising from a motive
and seeking a result—the type of action which always
requires the necessity of further action. Man is involved in
karma when he interferes with the world in such a way he is
compelled to go on interfering, when the solution of a
problem creates still more problems to be solved, when the
control of one thing creates the need to control several
others." [2]

There are two other ways to look at this that may help, *"You always thought it was a secret, but it never was,"* and *"What happens is exactly what was going to happen."* At first blush this may sound fatalist but consider these statements in the context of another said by Shunryu Suzuki, *"Each of you is perfect the way you are, but you can use a little improvement."*

Ultimately, karma is just a concept like any other concept, so don't get attached to it. Everything is a cause, and everything is an effect. Yet as Suzuki says the moment is complete and perfect as it is. Just as it is. When we meditate every breath is perfect just as it is, yet as you practice over time your practice leads to awakenings and gradual cultivation, awakenings and gradual cultivation. This is what we mean by the karmic step by step practice of Zen.

The Sangha

The third treasure is Sangha, from the Sanskrit word for assembly or community. In traditional Buddhism this usually means a community of monks (*bhikkhus*) or nuns (*bhikkunis*) but in Western Zen it has come to mean the community of priests, monks, nuns, teachers and lay members of a Zen center. It can also mean the larger community either of the entire group of Zen centers or of Zen as a whole—a so called "MahaSangha." And it can mean more than that, too: the even wider community of all sentient beings, every entity in the universe. When we vow to save all members of the sangha it is all members of this universal sangha we refer to. *Sentient beings are numberless, I vow to save them all.*

Here Zen plays one of its usual tricks, that I like to refer to as the impish nature of Zen teaching. The teaching that should ideally always be done with a smile and a glint in the teacher's eye. All beings are already saved, just as we are all already Buddhas. It is only an illusion that anyone needs to be saved, or that anyone needs to "become" a Buddha. This is how, although sentient beings are numberless, no action is required to save them all. Although, it may take a lifetime of practice to save even one.

Indra's Net

Indra's net is a fabulous metaphor found in the Atharva Veda and is reworked in Mahayana Buddhism in the 3rd century as part of the *Avatamaska Sutra*. The net is infinitely large and at every knot, or node, where the strands meet there is a brilliant multifaceted jewel that reflects all the other jewels in the net. While a beautiful metaphor for the entire universe, it is also an appropriate image for a Zen center's sangha. Each person in the Sangha is a jewel, reflecting every other jewel. This image also reflects the unique facets of the community and emphasizes the need to balance the needs of the entire group with the needs of each individual within the group. It is a complex relationship that needs to be held with compassion and infinite attention.

The Three Refuges

You will encounter this in many Zen centers, and it is central to Zen practice in most instances. It's called *The Three Refuges*:

I take refuge in the Buddha
I take refuge in the Dharma
I take refuge in the Sangha

The original Pali word translated as "refuge" is *saranam* which is a variation on the word that means "protection, shelter, to house, refuge." The meaning here is more of a vow than a simple statement of fact or faith. Yet in a sense as a set of vows it is an act of faith: the faith that by taking refuge in the three treasures one will realize one's true self. As Robert Aitken says:

> To realize the very heart of essential nature is to take refuge in the Buddha. To cultivate the garden of realization is to take refuge in the Dharma. To share the fruits of the garden is to take refuge in the Sangha. [3]

The Vinaya

I mention the Vinaya not because it is followed by many Western Zen centers, but because perhaps they might benefit from following it (or something like it). It is part of the Buddhist canon that deals with rules and procedures that govern Buddhist communities or sanghas. Chan Buddhism often followed the Vinaya but as Chan moved to Japan (and became known as Zen) the Vinaya was dropped. Essentially, the Vinaya is a very long list of what a monk or nun may or may not do in the monastery. It covers both the moral and ethical aspects of behavior and actions, as well as the practical day-to-day aspects of everyday life in a community.

I recall that when I introduced the idea to the Pasadena Zen Center that we might adopt some variation of the Vinaya, one of my students responded that he particularly liked rule number 57, which states "*I will not teach the Dharma to a person with an umbrella in his hand who is not ill.*"

Suffice to say, the Vinaya would need substantial overhaul before being put into everyday use in a Western Zen center. Many of the rules were applicable to uneducated monks several thousand years ago and are not relevant today. But in the meantime, the lack of clear sets of rules and guidelines may, in part, be responsible for some of the unacceptable behavior that has occurred at Zen centers in recent times. For now, centers do have some basic rules and most schools have what we call "The Precepts" that are an essential first step in formal training.

The Precepts

There are broad similarities to the precepts taken by Soto Zen students, and those taken in the Korean Zen tradition. Both also bear broad similarities to the Christian "Ten Commandments." One of the joys of working as a chaplain in a hospital is the quite marvelous people one meets. One such person I met was a strictly observant Orthodox Jew. He gently asked me, "*Do you know the difference between an Orthodox Jew and a Reform Jew?*" "*No,*" I replied, "*What is the difference?*"

"*Orthodox Jews have the Ten Commandments, whereas Reform Jews have the Ten Suggestions!*" Whereupon his entire body shook with the most delightful bout of laughing I have ever witnessed.

There is some parallel here, since whereas Christianity has its "commandments," Buddhism does not command obedience, rather it places the responsibility squarely on the student who is called to set mindful intentions to behave in certain ways.

Soto Sixteen Bodhisattva Precepts

In the Soto Zen tradition, students take what are known as the Sixteen Bodhisattva Precepts (*Kai*) during a ceremony known as *Jukai*. There are three components: The Three Treasures, the Three Pure Precepts and the Ten Grave Precepts.

We've already covered the Three Treasures, also known as the three jewels or the three refuges. These are the essence of our true nature. The Three Pure Precepts correspond to the order in which we function as the Three Treasures. Here is the version as taught at the Zen Center of Los Angeles, with its influence of Bernie Glassman's teachings:

- Do no evil (The Three Tenets, Not-Knowing)
- Do Good (The Three Tenets, Bearing Witness)
- Do Good for Others (The Three Tenets, Loving Action)

Finally, the Ten Grave Precepts that guide our functioning in daily life, living the Three Treasures. Here the word "grave" means the essential, or major precepts. Precept means a general rule intended to regulate behavior or thought, but here take on the form more of a vow. You will find a number of variations on the wording of these ten precepts, but here is one example (again from ZCLA):

1. Non-Killing
2. Non-Stealing
3. Not Being Greedy
4. Not Telling Lies
5. Not Being Ignorant
6. Not Talking about Others' Errors or Faults
7. Not Elevating Oneself and Blaming Others
8. Not Being Stingy
9. Not Being Angry

10. Not Speaking Ill of the Three Treasures

And for comparison, now from the *Brahmajala Sutra* (c 400 C.E.) which lists ten major vows and forty-eight minor vows:

1. Not to kill or encourage others to kill.
2. Not to steal or encourage others to steal.
3. Not to engage in licentious acts or encourage others to do so. A monk is expected to abstain from sexual conduct entirely.
4. Not to use false words and speech or encourage others to do so.
5. Not to trade or sell alcoholic beverages or encourage others to do so.
6. Not to broadcast the misdeeds or faults of the Buddhist assembly, nor encourage others to do so.
7. Not to praise oneself and speak ill of others or encourage others to do so.
8. Not to be stingy or encourage others to do so.
9. Not to harbor anger or encourage others to be angry.
10. Not to speak ill of the Buddha, the Dharma or the Sangha (the Triple Jewel) or encourage others to do so.

As you can see, this Zen center has decided to reframe the original admonitions against licentious behavior (No.3) with "Not Being Greedy," and against trading in alcohol (No.5) with "Not Being Ignorant." Each Zen center, or each branch of a lineage, has given a slightly different interpretation of the original vows mentioned in the sutras depending on their situation. Here, in ZCLA, is a center dealing with its history of a founder and leader who is associated with using alcohol in excess and indulging in licentious behavior.

In some centers you may find a more literal interpretation of the precepts being taught, in others a broader interpretation. For instance, one center's teachers may stay close to the wording of "Do Not Kill" by taking that both to mean don't kill other people and do not kill animals. They may thus promote a vegetarian or vegan diet, for instance, so as to adhere to this precept. Others may extend that to say yes don't kill other human beings or animals, but also don't kill another person's dreams, aspirations, or hopes.

Studying for the *Jukai* ceremony can take weeks, or even months, in some centers. One is mentored in the process by a preceptor, who is the priest or teacher who will be granting one the precepts at the ceremony. When receiving *Jukai* the student will also be given a dharma name, which in many cases is not intended to describe how the preceptor perceives the student at that time, but rather what the student should aspire to.

While studying for the precept ceremony, the Soto student will also likely be making a *rakusu*. This is a ceremonial robe that is worn round the neck, rather like a bib. Some will say it represents the Buddha's robe, others will be emphatic that it is the Buddha's robe in itself. Some centers may require that the student make such a *rakusu* from scratch, learning, if necessary, to sew such that stitches are hidden. For many, this task can be daunting, especially if they have never sown an item before. The task can be demanding not least if the Zen center you attend calls for a high level of accuracy so that the resulting *rakusu* looks professionally tailored, but not as if it was done by a machine. That said, it is usually more important the work be unique, and hence authentic, to that student, rather than being "perfect" (recalling Suzuki here). Many students report a tremendous sense of achievement when it is completed.

Where students are not required to make their own rakusu, then they are readily available for purchase online. In one center you may find the lay member's rakusu will be all black, whereas in another they may be another color such as dark blue. The Zen Peacemaker tradition started by Bernie Glassman introduced the idea of using pieces of cloth that have meaning to you (perhaps from clothing of your mother, father, spouse) dying it a dark maroon red, and using those pieces of cloth for the "rice field" main area of the front of the *rakusu*. While some centers (such as ZCLA) call for the resulting *rakusu* to be dark and muted, others permit the "peacemaker *rakusu*" to be highly colorful.

In some Japanese lineage Zen centers, once you have taken the precepts you may then wear lay robes, however, some centers may not permit the wearing robes by lay members. The lay robes are usually black and have fewer pleats and narrower sleeves than a more formal priest robe (which is also usually black). If permitted, the robes are generally for use when at the center, and in some instances, one will be asked to only wear them while inside the Zendo.

In contrast to the Soto Bodhisattva Precepts, Chan Buddhism and those paths that stayed closer to Chan (for example, Korean Zen), draw their precepts from the full text of the *Brahmajala Sutra*, rather than just the ten major vows.

Thus, a student may initially take just five precepts whereupon they will attend a ceremony at which they received a dharma name as well as a *wagesa*—a ceremonial cloth with tassels at the end, resembling a small stole. Usually, this first one will be blue, and it represents the vast blue empty sky, and is to be worn over lay clothing. Generally, one takes these initial five precepts when one is ready to do so, and when one has usually had at least six months of regular practice with their Precepts Teacher. Here are the Five Precepts:

1. I vow to support all living creatures, and refrain from killing.
2. I vow to respect the property of others, and refrain from stealing.
3. I vow to regard all beings with respect and dignity, and refrain from objectifying others.
4. I vow to be truthful, and refrain from lying.
5. I vow to maintain a clear mind and refrain from harming myself or others with intoxication.

The next step for the more serious student would be to take the eight precepts and become an *Anagarika* or *Anagariya*. Sometimes this will come with a calling to help the sick, the poor, the marginalized, or those imprisoned. At this level the student receives a green *wagesa*, and at the ceremony takes these further three precepts in addition to the prior five precepts:

The Sixth Precept: I vow to be kind to others and refrain from being boastful and self-centered.

The Seventh Precept: I vow to be generous, to be grateful for what I have, and refrain from yearning for things that do not belong to me.

The Eighth Precept: I vow to promote harmony and refrain from acting in anger or hatred.

If so called, and if approved by one's teacher, a student might go on to become a Novice Monk (*Sramanera/Sramaneri*). This student takes the ten precepts (two further ones beyond the last stage) and wears a green *Bangasa* over pale grey robes, representing the new growth of plants. These are the additional two precepts one takes at this ceremony:

The Ninth Precept: I vow to promote harmony and refrain from acting in anger or hatred.

The Tenth Precept: I vow to affirm and uphold the three jewels (the Buddha, the Sangha and the Dharma).

If the student is then called to become *Brahmajala Priest*, the student will take fifty-eight precepts, and wear a brown full *gasa* representing solid trunks of large trees (full cloak-like outer robe) worn over their pale grey robe. These further forty-eight vows may be as follows (this version from the Five Mountain Zen Center):

11. I vow to respect my teachers and friends in the Dharma
12. I vow to abstain from entering into intoxicating situations or consuming substances intended to distract from this moment.
13. I vow to be conscious of what I consume, the way in which it was produced, and what harm might result from my consuming it. I vow to bring awareness to the impact of what I ingest and take care not to harm myself or any other beings in the process.
14. I vow to maintain the integrity and sanctity of the teacher/clergy to student relationship by never entering into a sexual or otherwise inappropriate relationship and thereby violating the trust of the student as well as the entire sangha.
15. I vow to encourage others to view past mistakes as learning opportunities that enable them to make better choices in the future.
16. I vow to always request the Dharma and make offerings to visiting Sangha members
17. I vow to attend Dharma talks and events that will open my heart and mind; thus enabling my practice to grow stronger and allowing me to be of better service

to others.

18. I vow not to divide the Dharma into separate vehicles or doctrines by placing one classification as higher or better than another.

19. I vow to always give care to the sick and the needy

20. I vow to abstain from the storing of weapons used to intentionally take away life.

21. I vow to abstain from serving as an emissary of the military, except in non-violent roles such as Chaplaincy, Medical Positions, and other roles that do not directly engage in the violent expression of military service.

22. I vow to conduct my livelihood in a way that that is helpful to myself and others and refrain from business practices that limit the freedom or happiness of others.

23. I vow to communicate in a way that is true, accurate and helpful and to refrain from speech meant to plant seeds of doubt, misinformation, or gossip.

24. I vow to support life by behaving in a way that respects and protects the environment as well as all beings and to refrain from activities that may cause harm.

25. I vow to teach the Dharma in a manner that inspires awakening and well-being for myself and others.

26. I vow to fully understand the Dharma so that I may teach it in a manner that is true, accurate, and helpful.

27. I vow to share the Dharma as freely as I have received it, with no personal gain as my motive.

28. I vow to serve others with commitment, kindness,

and integrity.

29. I vow to communicate in a direct and compassionate manner that promotes harmony and to refrain from speech that contains hidden or implied messages meant to cause harm or unhappiness.

30. I vow to liberate all sentient beings from suffering and the causes of suffering.

31. I vow to treat others with respect and to refrain from behaving in a manner that violates, harms, or imposes revenge on others.

32. I vow to conduct myself in a manner that is consistent with the Dharma: to remain humble and accessible and to refrain from arrogant or self-important behavior.

33. I vow to teach the Dharma with generosity and an open heart

34. I vow to put the teachings of the Buddha-Dharma into practice in my everyday life and to teach others how to do the same.

35. I vow to be a Sangha member that acts with integrity and accountability.

36. I vow to share all offerings made to the Dharma or the Sangha

37. I vow to accept invitations given equally to all others and refrain from accepting invitations that exclude anyone based on gender, race, religion, physical condition, age, or sexual orientation.

38. I vow to be inclusive and to invite all people equally regardless of gender, race, religion, physical condition, or sexual orientation.

39. I vow to conduct my livelihood in a way that that is helpful to myself and others and refrain from business practices that limit the freedom or happiness of others.

40. I vow to give all Sangha members equal consideration and respect and to refrain from engaging in any actions that might cause division or conflict.

41. I vow respect all clergy members and Dharmic objects.

42. I vow to extend loving-kindness indiscriminately to all sentient beings, and to greet all experiences with openness, curiosity, and acceptance.

43. I vow to approach all beings with respect and dignity and refrain from objectifying others.

44. I vow to always keep a clear and open mind.

45. I vow to make great vows

46. I vow to make firm resolutions

47. I vow to keep myself safe whenever possible and to refrain from putting myself or others in environments where harm is more likely.

48. I vow to respect all members of the Sangha equally.

49. I vow to cultivate wisdom and good judgment.

50. I vow not to unfairly discriminate against others when conferring the precepts.

51. I vow equanimity in teaching the Dharma and will not to enter into teaching arrangements for the sake of profit.

52. I vow to offer the precepts only to those that wish to take them with an sincere and open heart.

53. I vow to uphold all of these precepts.

54. I vow to value the Sutras and the ethical guidelines set forth by the Buddha.

55. I vow to teach and serve all sentient beings in ways that are appropriate for who they are.

56. I vow to teach the Dharma in ways that are appropriate and helpful and to refrain from teaching in ways that cause harm.

57. I vow to consistently support the Dharma in my daily life.

58. I vow to keep the Dharma fresh, alive, and vibrant and to refrain from any actions that might cause its destruction.

Alternatively, becoming a monk (*Bhiksu/Bhijsuni*) in this tradition requires that one take the 250 Monastic Precepts, and also wear a brown *kesa* over formal long pale grey robes.

Robe Colors

Briefly, Japanese Zen traditions—both Soto and Rinzai—call for black robes to be worn by lay members, priests, monks, nuns and teachers. The hierarchy is then further defined by the color of the *rakusu* or the *kesa* that is worn over the basic black robes. The *kesa* is an outer robe, or over-robe, usually worn over the left shoulder, and under the right shoulder. Priests will usually wear a black *kesa* whereas teachers (*sensei*) wear a dark brown *kesa* and those with full dharma transmission wear a lighter ochre color *kesa*.

In the Vietnam Zen (Thien) tradition the robes are usually grey for novices and mid-brown for those fully ordained. If they wear a gasa, then it is usually yellow. In the Korean Zen (Seon) tradition they are usually light gray. There a growing number of centers and branches of Zen that permit students, priests and teachers greater latitude to wear different color robes and *kesas*—particularly where the branch of Zen has more than one lineage or members who have been ordained in more than one lineage or tradition. There can also be wide variation in the color of *rakusus* worn, tradition to tradition, center to center, and then variation of those colors within the center or tradition to indicate rank and position.

---

[1] You may find some sources use the word "right" instead of "correct."

[2] Alan Watts, *The Way of Zen*, The New American Library, 1957, 58.

[3] Robert Aitken, *Taking the Path of Zen*, North Point Press, 1982, 76.

Good and bad come from your own mind. But what do you call your own mind, apart from your actions and thoughts? Where does your own mind come from? If you really know where you own mind comes from, boundless obstacles caused by your own actions will be cleared all at once. After seeing that, all sorts of extraordinary possibilities will come to you without your seeking them.

Chan Master Dahui Zonggao

six

The Ten Oxherding Pictures

The Ten Oxherding Pictures are a traditional Chinese collection of art and poems that depict the Zen path to awakening. If you visit Zen temples in China, Korea, or Japan you will see these images on the walls. In these images we see a young oxherder who finds the ox, then tames it, and brings it home. Most importantly, the final image is going back out into the world. An awakened bodhisattva goes back into society to help others. The true self is "How may I help you?"

1. **In Search of the Ox**

In the pasture of the world, I endlessly push aside the tall grasses in search of the Ox. Following unnamed rivers, lost upon the interpenetrating paths of distant mountains.

My strength failing and my vitality exhausted, I cannot find the Ox.

You are still in confusion, because of karmic bonds. You have heard that there is something marvelous but have never seen it. You would like to search for it, but do not know how. Where is the path?

2. Discovery of the Footprints

Along the riverbank under the trees, I discover footprints.
Even under the fragrant grass, I see his prints.
Deep in remote mountains they are found. These traces can no more be hidden than one's nose, looking heavenward

The path is becoming clear. You anticipate the opening of the path, and the understanding of what has hitherto been mystery. You are eager to find and tread the path! What shall my practice be?

3. Perceiving the Ox

I hear the song of the nightingale. The sun is warm, the wind is mild, willows are green along the shore - Here no Ox can hide! What artist can draw that massive head, those majestic horns?

Practice brings you fleeting glimpses of "original mind." You experience nano seconds of freedom from illusion of self, and the duality it spawns. You do not merely suspect that freedom exists, but you do not have it yet.

113

4. Catching the Ox

I seize him with a terrific struggle. His great will and power are inexhaustible.
He charges to the high plateau far above the cloud-mists,
Or in an impenetrable ravine he stands.

Your karmic bonds – desire, attachment, weak intentions – bring about a terrific struggle as you try to maintain original mind. Will dualism do you in, as you paradoxically try to hold on to letting go?

5. Taming the Ox

The whip and rope are necessary, else he might stray off down some dusty road.
Being well-trained, he becomes naturally gentle.
Then, unfettered, he obeys his master.

Diligence – right effort – has deepened your practice, and now we must remain relaxed but alert, at-ease but awake. Constant diligence is needed now.
Dare you take the ox off the tether?

6. Riding the Ox Home

Mounting the Ox, slowly I return homeward. The voice of my flute intones through the evening. Measuring with hand-beats the pulsating harmony, I direct the endless rhythm. Whoever hears this melody will join me.

Your everyday mind is carried by original mind, not vice versa. Realization is displacing views and intentions. Dualism is not yet gone, but can you walk the talk?

7. The Ox Transcended

Astride the Ox, I reach home.
I am serene. The Ox too can rest.
The dawn has come. In blissful repose,
Within my thatched dwelling
I have abandoned the whip and ropes.

Thich Naht Hanh has said, "I have arrived, I am home, in the here, and the now."
Being fully present, what is the need for the duality of "everyday mind" vs. "original mind?"

8. Both Ox and Self Transcended

Whip, rope, person, and Ox - all merge in No Thing. This heaven is so vast, no message can stain it. How may a snowflake exist in a raging fire? Here are the footprints of the Ancestors.

Sunyata. In the words of the Heart Sutra...
"...all phenomena bear the mark of Emptiness.
their true nature is the nature of no Birth no Death, no Being no Non-being, no Defilement no Purity, no Increasing no Decreasing.
... the Path, insight and attainment,
are also not separate-self entities.
Whoever can see this no longer
needs anything to attain.

9. Reaching the Source

Too many steps have been taken returning to the root and the source. Better to have been blind and deaf from the beginning! Dwelling in one's true abode, unconcerned with and without - The river flows tranquilly on and the flowers are red.

Now, here in the present moment, will you maintain freedom from the duality of original mind and everyday mind?

"Sitting quietly, doing nothing, Spring comes, and the grass grows, by itself." (Basho, Japanese Zen poet.)

10. In the Marketplace with Helping Hands

Barefooted and naked of chest,
I mingle with the people of the world. My clothes are ragged and
dust-laden, and I am ever blissful. I use no magic to extend my
life; Now, before me, the dead trees become alive

*Bodhisattva! You have become the ox, unselfconsciously taking
dharma fruits into the world for all beings.*

To study the Buddha Way is to study the self. To study the self is to forget the self. To forget the self is to be actualized by myriad things. When actualized by myriad things, your body and mind as well as the bodies and minds of others drop away. No trace of awakening remains, and this no-trace continues endlessly.

Dogen

seven

The Zen Way

To follow the Zen way is to become a fool—but not just any fool, a very special kind of fool. Awakening is simply a matter of realizing who we are, nothing special, it's even called "ordinary mind" in Zen circles. How hard can that be? Well, apparently very hard since so few people pass through the gateless gate. Here you are, a unique point at which the universe becomes aware of itself, and yet the simple act of living fully in this moment seems beyond us.

But this moment is the only moment there is—what we call the "past" and the "future" are illusions we have invented—so if we can't live in this moment, we can't truly live at all. Why is this Zen path so hard to follow? It isn't because it is hard to sit for hours staring at a wall, or hard to have interviews with your teacher to work on koans. Yes, they can both *seem* hard at times, but they aren't the problem. It is our inability to keep our minds focused that makes this path so hard.

A key part of the problem is the temptation to think that by sitting or by working on koans you will "gain" awakening. It is so alien to most of us that what we are called to do by Zen is simply drop it all. Put it all down. We talk about "gaining mind" in Zen, and it means our practice needs to be without thought of gaining something from it. But this doesn't mean you sit with no purpose: that would be like randomly hitting keys on your keyboard and trusting that by pure chance you will produce a best-selling novel.

Nowhere is this more obvious than when one tries to stop one's mind during zazen. We talk of stopping the mind, but if you actively try to stop your thoughts then you fall into a basic trap. Trying to stop your thoughts is dualistic thinking—me distinct from these "thoughts" that are separate from "me" and can be controlled or corralled by "me." Your goal, insofar as you have a goal in Zen practice, is that your sitting be effortless. And this is where persistence and discipline come in.

One way we talk about this is to say in Christianity you might pray as you peel potatoes, using your time doing chores as an opportunity to pray. In Zen we say when peeling potatoes, just peel the potatoes. As it happens, there could be no deeper prayer, but that's a topic for a different book.[1] As simple as it sounds, just doing what we are doing with one hundred percent attention is very difficult for most people.

When the Japanese founder of the Soto branch of Chan, Dogen, spoke of "just sitting" (*shikantaza*) many misunderstand and believe he is just espousing wall-gazing meditation—"If you sit you will become enlightened"—but no, it is a call to just sit when you sit. This is the effortless sitting, not sitting that is filled with a flood of monkey mind thoughts, distraction of discomfort and pain, frustration at the noise someone else in the room makes. That is all dualistic mind: the mind of form is form and emptiness is emptiness. One needs to move on to perceive form is emptiness, emptiness is form and there is non-dual effortless sitting.

There is a school of thought that zazen is something you only do when sitting on a cushion in the zendo, or a dedicated room set aside for sitting zazen. But zazen when perfected is done wherever you are, whether sitting, standing, lying down, working, playing, resting. Yet, zazen like any other practice takes persistence and dedication, you don't perfect this skill any quicker than, say, perfecting running a marathon. When first starting zazen, you may find you have difficulty breathing. It may almost seem embarrassing that just sitting in total silence causes you to somehow forget how to breath properly. This is the centipede's dilemma:

> A centipede was happy – quite!
> Until a toad in fun
> Said, "Pray, which leg comes after which?"
> Which threw her mind in such a pitch,
> She laid bewildered in the ditch
> Considering how to run.

If you experience this, don't worry, it's not at all unusual at first to become self-conscious about basic processes like breathing. For others it is swallowing, they find saliva building up in their mouth as they sit because they are "forgetting" to swallow. Zazen can be an excellent litmus test for the mind: if you can sit and *just sit*, breathing normally, you have taken an important first step toward effortless sitting. A lucky few have no such problems from the beginning, others start with no problems and then as their sitting deepens the issues arise: "*That tickle in my throat! But they said not to cough in the zendo...*"; "*Oh no, now my face is itching, should I scratch it? Will someone be annoyed if I move my hand?*"

Some effort is necessary to get past any such initial issues, but above all be gentle on yourself. You will get to a point where zazen is effortless, but it will take time and patience. Remember, the best way to make cloudy water clear is to just leave it alone.

Flail in the water and you will drown, relax and you will float

Zen is not about learning something, it is about unlearning. You will be surprised just how many habits, beliefs, constructs and assumptions you have acquired in the few years you have been alive. Whether you are eighteen or ninety-eight, you have accumulated a huge number of deep-rooted ideas about who you are and what the universe is all about. Take your basic everyday view of the world: looking around the room you are in, it is full of color, right? Now look straight ahead without moving your head and notice the room to your left and to your right. Far left, far right. You don't feel you are in a room that is a mix of color and monochrome, right?

But the fact is you see color with the center of your eyes, whereas your peripheral vision is attuned to perceiving move-ment. It makes sense in evolutionary terms since being able to see detail and colors is more important in the center of your visual field that you are focused on. Whereas it is more important that you be aware of someone or something creeping up on you, so movement sensors are more important at the edges of your sight.

Yet you don't perceive the world as being color dead ahead of you and grey everywhere else, rather you live in a colorful world. This is because your brain is filling in the color and creating your perception of a world that has continuity and coherence. Where coherence doesn't exist (in the sense of actual perceptual data being received by the brain), the brain fills in the gaps.

It is well known that eyewitnesses are notoriously unreliable. Five people seeing the same person commit the same act have been known to give five quite different accounts. Person one expected to see someone of a specific demographic and so that is what they see. Person two expected to see a different kind of person, and so that is what they see. There is a video on the Internet of some people playing with a ball. Over and again, when asked to watch the video and count the number of times the ball bounces people have the same reaction. They are totally stunned to learn that while they watched the ball, a man in a gorilla suit had walked across the screen, totally unnoticed by them. On replaying the video, they find it hard to believe they missed such an obvious thing the first viewing.

More often than we realize, we see what we expect to see rather than some raw unprocessed perception of the world just as it really is. Perhaps you've had an experience in twilight hours when you see a dog in the leaves beneath the tree, only to then realize what you are looking at is just the wind churning up the leaves.

Again, this makes sense that our brain makes stuff up: every millisecond thousands of new pieces of sense data enter our senses. We can't handle processing absolutely every piece of sense data, and it isn't necessary for us to function in the world that we do so. Indeed, as the autistic person can attest, if you do try to process all your sense data you can freeze up with processing overload.

We can liken beginner's mind to the mind of a child. A child who is still filled with wonder and hasn't been conditioned by society to see this but not that, to think this but not that, to react this way but not that way, etc. But to become functioning adults we must become conditioned, we have to develop both conceptions and preconceptions because they help us to stay safe, to survive. If having touched a hot stove burner and felt the pain we do not develop a concept of "glowing stove burners are hot" then we keep touching the burner, keep getting burnt.

That may sound trivial, but it isn't. Such concepts and preconceptions can be practical, but they can also be perfidious and insidious. We need to learn that objects that get larger and larger are coming toward us. If we fail to integrate this into our basic perception of the world then we get run over by the Mack truck. But these concepts and preconceptions are at their most subtle and tricky when it comes to the ego.

Now, you may have been told that Zen is all about "destroying your ego," but this is nonsense. It depends what you mean by the word "ego" of course, but regardless, nothing about this practice involves destruction of ego. If you mean your sense of self as a separate being, separate from all other beings, then your path includes recognizing that this is a delusion. But if you mean the "me" who says while standing in the middle of the road, *"That shape coming toward me is getting larger every moment,"* then you had certainly better not destroy it. Remember the Mack truck.

In this moment you are absolutely finite and small, but you are also infinite and limitless. This is the form and the emptiness we discussed before. But form is emptiness—it is all you, the finite and the infinite. You are x-feet, y-inches tall (the *relative*); and you are no size at all, you are infinitely large (the *absolute*). Realizing this calls for cultivating a pure mind. This pure mind is the beginner's mind (*shoshin* in Japanese), it is to be constantly saying to yourself *"What is this? Don't know."* It is holding a don't know mind, it is dwelling in non-dualism when the entirety of our life seems to scream for us to dwell in dualism.

If you seek Zen on the top of a mountain, then the only Zen you'll find there is the Zen you brought with you. Similarly, you will be disappointed if you attend a Zen center and assume that act alone will give you awakening, any more than the act of signing up for membership of a gym will improve your fitness. Much of the problem is the basic teaching of Zen is that you need to wake up, but you don't understand that concept: "*Surely I'm already awake? I woke up this morning, and have been awake all day ever since, haven't I?*" As hard as it may be to envisage going to sleep and never waking up, how much harder is it to imagine waking up when you never fell asleep?

There is a good reason why when someone experiences an awakening experience—a *kensho*—it can be accompanied by a feeling of elation, light-headedness, even ecstasy. Now, here lies the danger: having experienced that moment, having felt ecstatic, you can then be tempted to spend years trying to "get back" to *that* experience. The seduction, the error, is to believe that the "high" you experience in an awakening moment is the goal. The mistake is thinking that this is the feeling a fully awakened person experiences all the time. This way lies the danger of being attracted to mind altering substances since they may be a way of recreating such "highs," but they are an illusion and take one further and further away from realizing your true self.

In Zen it's said that being awake is as grey as grey. I sometimes feel teachers say that to set student expectation and dissuade them from either believing the goal of Zen is to "get high." Of course, saying the ultimate goal is an utterly grey world view is hardly a great selling point! Indeed, it isn't true:

when awake, grey is just grey, startling red is just startling red, pain is pain—but it isn't suffering. Ecstasy is ecstasy—but it isn't seductive.

For many, having a *kensho* experience, a momentary glimpse of awakening, is as much a curse as a gift. If it leads to a belief that the initial buzz you got is the state you need to return to, then indeed it can be a curse since that is not what awakening is all about. It can also be dispiriting: I have lost count of the people who have said to me, "*I had what I thought was a kensho experience many years ago, but I've never been able to get it again.*"

Yet, it's understandable why some branches of Soto Zen hold having at least one initial *kensho* experience as central to a student's path. For most, the words spoken in Zen are simply nonsense until one experiences at least a glimpse of awakening: then it all starts to make sense. An "*Ah ha!*" moment happens for most and this is the point it can be so very important that a student of Zen has a teacher or mentor to guide them through processing the experience. Without such guidance, it can be easy to fall into the trap that the emotions felt are seen as the main goal of Zen that must be experienced again.

When all else falls away, what remains is compassion

I do not recommend playing the game of "spot the enlightened being," but should you be tempted to look for someone who is on the path, then do not look for the person always happy, always laughing (even when sad events occur), but rather look for that person with a gentle smile, one who laughs heartily when appropriate, and cries freely when appropriate, has an unassuming air, an unselfish nature, and a presence of equanimity—nothing seems to unsettle them. I'd say, *"Look for the person who keeps their head when all around have lost theirs,"* but that would not sit well with my dear friend and mentor, Douglas Harding (much missed), whose unique Zen teaching was to help you realize that you have no head.[2]

Your true nature is compassion: may you realize it.

---

[1] Tim Langdell, *Christ Way, Buddha Way: Jesus as Wisdom Teacher and a Zen Perspective on His Teachings*, StillCenter Publications, 2020; Tim Langdell, *Kenosis: Christian Self-Emptying Meditation*, StillCenter Publications, 2020.

[2] Douglas Harding, *On Having No Head: a Contribution to Zen in the West*, Harper & Row, 1972. Or the more recent edition *On Having No Head: Zen and the Rediscovery of the Obvious*, The Sholland Trust, 2013.

In this very breath
that we take now
lies the secret that
all great teachers
try to tell us.

Peter Matthiessen

eight

Zen Practice

Whether you follow the Zen way as a casual lay practitioner based in your own home, or more seriously at a formal Zen center, meditation will be at the core of your practice. If you are drawn to pursue Zen more deeply you may attend retreats lasting anywhere from a day to as much as three months, or you may also do koan introspection work with a teacher.

Meditation (zazen)

In the Maha-satipatthana Sutra (DN 22), Buddha mentions four positions for mediation: walking, standing, sitting and lying down. However, he also went on to clarify that when meditating "one makes oneself fully alert." For this reason, you will find lying down meditation is rarely practiced at Zen centers in the West since it is harder to remain fully awake and alert when lying down. Most Zen centers and sitting groups will practice zazen (sitting meditation) and some will also practice walking meditation—known as *kinhin* in Japanese.

Here is what Dogen, the founder of the Japanese Soto Zen tradition, had to say about sitting zazen:

"For zazen, a quiet room is suitable. Eat and drink moderately. Cast aside all involvements and cease all affairs. Do not think good or bad. Do not administer pros and cons. Cease all the movements of the conscious mind, the gauging of all thoughts and views. Have no designs on becoming a Buddha. Zazen has nothing whatever to do with sitting or lying down.

At the site of your regular sitting, spread out thick matting and place a cushion above it. Sit either in the Full Lotus or Half Lotus position. In the Full Lotus position, you first place your right foot on your left thigh and your left foot on your right thigh. In the Half Lotus, you simply press your left foot against your right thigh. You should have your robes and belt loosely bound and arranged in order. Then place your right hand on your left leg and your left palm [facing upward] on your right palm, thumb-tips touching.

Thus, sit upright in correct bodily posture, neither inclining to the left nor to the right, neither leaning forward nor backward. Be sure your ears are on a plane with your shoulders and your nose in line with your navel. Place your tongue against the front roof of your mouth, with teeth and lips both shut. Your eyes should always remain open, and you should breathe gently through your nose."

Sitting zazen at home

Even if you sit regularly on a weekly basis at a Zen center or a local sitting group, it is highly advisable that you also set up a daily practice for yourself. Ideally you should be aiming to sit at least twice a day, morning and evening, but some practitioners will sit midday, too, and others will sit only once a day. Establishing a routine that you can adhere to is very important. For this reason, I do not recommend pushing yourself beyond what you are comfortable doing, since doing less on a regular basis is more important than doing more but sporadically. So, first determine how long you intend to sit for and how many times a day.

Second, establish a place you will do your practice: at home, if you can, set aside an area where you can be in quiet and not disturbed. By all means, do whatever you feel comfortable doing to make this area a "sacred space." What that means is entirely up to you: for many it is having a zabuton and zafu (padded mat and sitting cushion) on the floor, and for others it may be a meditation stool or chair. For some, it is creating an altar or a table with some calming items on it such as a statue of Buddha, incense bowl, and perhaps a small flower arrangement. If one does have an image of Buddha then please remember he is not an idol to be worshiped, so any statue is to remind one of the first of the three treasures and of one's true nature.

On a practical note, you will want to identify a way to time your sessions. For most of us these days this involves using the timer on our smart phone, or an app that can both time a session and have gentle sounds such as bells or bowls to mark the start and end of the period. Wearing relaxing clothing can also be useful and you may wish to explore the variety of meditation and yoga clothing on sale to see if something in particular works for you.

Of course, your middle of the day session, if that is part of your daily routine, may be at work or somewhere else you have less control over where you can meditate. If possible, try to still find somewhere quiet away from others. But just go with what is possible—I have had students who are nurses or doctors and who do their midday session at their computer stations on the ward or in their breakroom. Others can leave their place of work and go to a nearby park, or some other place more conducive to sitting in silence. Whatever works for you.

Unlike other forms of meditation, Zen does not involve repeating a word or phrase to yourself. The purpose of zazen is to be fully awake and alert in the moment, and a single word can fill your being and completely distract you from this moment. For this reason, we do not use words while practicing zazen and it is the reason we employ *all* the senses and do not close our eyes. The other reason we do not close our eyes is that this leads to a greater tendency to doze off, have a waking dream, or to just drift.

That said, we do not keep our eyes wide open either. Rather, you should have your eyes about half open, look roughly forty-five degrees down, and hold a soft gaze. This soft gaze is slightly unfocused, rather than focusing sharply on a spot on the floor or whatever is in front of you, since the idea is not to be concentrating on an object or a specific spot but rather to be fully open to all the senses. Here I am reminded of a story told by Zen teacher James Ford. He recounts how a student bounded up to him at an event and thanked him profusely for teaching her many years earlier how to mediate. "*I never forgot what you told me,*" she said, "*Hold a soft gaze and look intently at a spot on the floor.*" No, not that!

How you sit is important. The overriding consideration is that you sit comfortably in a way that, for you, remains comfortable for extended periods of time. In Zen we talk about "sitting like a mountain." You should sit so as to promote being fully awake, and for this reason you will need to sit upright, spine straight but comfortably so (don't sit such that you are straining to keep your back straight).

Your shoulders should be relaxed, and your head upright but tilted forward slightly (chin in) so that your gaze can naturally fall about forty-five degrees down. It may help to imagine a string attached to the center of the top of your head as if someone is pulling very gently on it to keep your head upright without straining to do so.

Next, we come to what you sit on, in what posture, and how you hold your hands. Dogen wrote as if there were only two possible postures—full lotus and half lotus. Indeed, because of the influence of eastern practices, you may associate sitting for meditation as being crossed legged, on a cushion on the floor. In the East, sitting on the floor crossed legged is a cultural norm in most societies. In the West this is less common since many of us are used to sitting on a chair. You will encounter those in the

Zen world who insist that "proper" zazen can only be done on a cushion one the floor. But if you need to sit on a chair, that can work well, too. Here are a number of commonly used postures:

If you are sitting crossed legged on a cushion, then there are some scientific reasons why if you're able to cross your legs fully that can help you sit longer without back pain. You may have heard this being called "full lotus" (the first image on the left above). It does have the advantage of creating a more perfect stable triangle to help your posture during a longer period of contemplation. Second best is to cross one leg over the other (so called "half lotus"), and next best is to tuck the legs in with each other as in the upper right image (so called "Burmese" posture).

Others find kneeling to be the best for them. You can kneel on your legs but be aware this can lead to your legs "going to sleep" because you're cutting off circulation to them. It is better to either kneel using a small stool to support you (see the lower left image above) or perhaps on a cushion that is placed on its side (lower middle image). Last, there is the position in which some in the West feel most comfortable, sitting in a chair.

If you are sitting on a cushion, then you should sit on the edge of it so that you're using a forty-five-degree angle of the cushion edge to create a more natural arch to your lower back. This also helps keep your chest open, and generally helps you feel more relaxed. As I mentioned above, your shoulders should be relaxed, drawn slightly back and down. Your chin should be tucked in a little—as with other aspects of your posture, you may wish to experiment with what works best for you. Your jaw should be free of tension so check that you are not clenching your teeth. Your tongue should be gently resting on the roof of your mouth, tip touching the back of the upper teeth. Finally, if sitting in a chair then your feet should be shoulder width apart, legs at a right angle to the floor, feet flat on the floor.

Returning to the question of your gaze for a moment— ideally you should have your eyes about half open, looking with a soft gaze about forty-five-degrees down. But if you find that, at least at first, you can relax better with your eyes closed then do so. Ideally, in time, if you do start with your eyes closed then open them halfway as soon as you can. Consider closing your eyes at all as being a kind of "training wheels" to stop using as soon as you're able. Again, our goal with zazen is to become fully awake, to adopt beginner's mind, to realize your buddha-nature. For zazen we hold our hands in the *cosmic mudra* position.

The hands are held around the navel level, and you will notice some practitioners have a small cushion they use to rest their hands on—this can be useful for a longer sitting session. First hold your left hand out, palm up. Then place the middle knuckle of the middle finger of your right hand face up on the middle of the middle finger of your left hand (as shown above). Then rest your two thumbs gently together.

Some instructors say the thumbs should be so lightly touching that someone should be able to walk around and pass a thin piece of paper through the thumbs with no resistance. Placing the hands in this position can have a useful purpose, since if you should start to drift off during zazen you will notice your thumbs have drifted apart and can bring them back together. Others have reported that if they get too tense then they can notice this by the thumbs pressing too hard against each other and adjust accordingly.

Unlike some yoga-based meditation practices, zazen does not call for deep breathing but rather encourages natural breaths. Breathing through the nose is recommended, without controlling it in any way. That said, it can be beneficial to breathe from your sola plexus (lower abdomen), this way your breathing can be deeper but still natural. This has some similarity to yogic breathing, with the in-breath filling the lower abdomen, and then exhaling completely so that the diaphragm is fully relaxed. It's sometimes referred to as belly breathing in contrast to more shallow breathing from the upper chest.

Sometimes you will hear zazen referred to as "wall-gazing." In some traditions meditating while facing a wall is the norm. But in various Zen traditions you may find either that practitioners sit facing into the room (toward each other), or that a session of zazen starts with wall-gazing and then transitions to facing into the room. While practicing on your own, you will find what works best for you. With no one else in the room, the decision will be largely one of how distracting your visual field is.

In some Zen centers—Soto Zen in particular—you may find that practitioners who have received *jukai*, and thus have their rakusu, do not put it on at first. The group will sit initially facing the wall with their rakusu on their *zabuton* to their side. Or, in the case of teachers and priests, with the outer robe (*kesa*) on the mat. Then after the initial period of sitting, someone will start the "Verse of the Kesa:"

> *Vast is the robe of liberation,*
> *a formless field of benefaction.*
> *I wear the Tathagata-teaching*
> *serving all sentient beings.*

As this is chanted, the practitioner will place their folded *rakusu* or *kesa* on their head, and then after a few moments will remove it, unfold it, and place it on themselves. In some centers, this will also be the moment that they switch from wall-gazing, to turn their chair or their position on the cushion to face inwards. What is done in the center you attend may differ, and I can only advise you gain clear instruction from a teacher since in some centers it can be seen as important to get this right. Practitioners who do not have a *rakusu* or *kesa* still chant still the verse and change the meditation position in synchrony with everyone else.

Sitting etiquette usually includes the manner in which you start your zazen session. Each center will have its own rules and guidance about how one acts within the meditation space, or *zendo*. For instance, you may find requests not to walk in front of the altar while entering and going to your cushion. It may be that you are to walk around the edge of the space, rather than across the center of it. Yet other meetings, especially if they are not in a formal *zendo*, may be far more relaxed with such rules.

 If one has carried one's cushion into the *zendo* or meditation room, then one places it carefully on the *zabuton*, smoothing out any wrinkles in either the mat or the cushion. If one is not carrying anything, then one should be walking into the zendo with hands in sassho (some centers will ask you walk with hands in gassho). Then one does a standing bow, hands in gassho, leaning just slightly forward as one bows. Next, one turns to face the room and does a slight bow again, still in

gassho. As the rest of the practitioners gather it may be the center's practice to stand at the edge of your mat, facing into the room, hands now in sassho (right hand over left with right thumb held in left hand). As the person opposite you

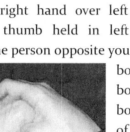 bows, it is usual to return the bow—hands return to gassho, bow, then back to sassho. And of course, if you have a *rakusu* you will have your hands in sassho behind your *rakasu*.

As to which cushion or chair one is to sit on, each center will have its own guidelines and rules for such matters. In some cases, they will tell you to enter the meditation hall, bow in the direction of the altar (slight bow, hands in gassho), then walk to the nearest vacant cushion of chair. "Vacant" will mean not just not currently being used but one that does not have someone's items on it, saving the spot. In some centers you will stand in sassho waiting for others to arrive before sitting, in other centers you will sit immediately having first bowed to your cushion and then to the room.

Of course, before entering the meditation hall you will have removed your shoes, and in some cases, you will be required to remove socks, too. You step into the hall, left foot first (leaving, you step right foot first). If you arrive late, some centers will require you to bow, and take just one step into the hall and then bow to the directing monk (*jikijitsu*), or other person who appears to be in charge of *zendo* procedure. That person will indicate if its appropriate for you to enter, and where you should go. In some Zen centers, entering once the meditation session has started is forbidden and you must wait until everyone is doing the waling meditation to enter, whereupon when you do so you seamlessly join those walking, merging without causing anyone to have to alter their step or pace.

In some centers a standard sitting session will comprise of two sessions of sitting—often about forty minutes long—with a period of walking meditation (*kinhin*) in between. One will receive the indication by the head monk ringing a bell to mark the end of the sitting session. At this point, you stand, and this is what Dogen said about standing at this point:

> *When you arise from sitting, move slowly and quietly, calmly and deliberately. Do not rise suddenly or abruptly. In surveying the past, we find that transcendence of both unenlightenment and enlightenment, and dying while either sitting or standing, have all depended entirely on the strength of zazen.*

Having stood, it is usual to stand in sassho for a moment until the head monk makes a sound with wooden clappers. At this one then turns a quarter turn (usually to the left, clockwise, in Chinese and Japanese *zendos*, but Korean centers they turn to the right, anticlockwise). The clappers are struck again, and one starts walking very slowly, gaze down around forty-five degrees as they were when sitting. There is variation center to center, but often the steps in Soto will be very slow—a single short step per breath.

In Rinzai centers, the walking may be moderately brisk. In some Soto centers one starts walking very slowly and then after a period of a few minutes the clappers strike again (twice, usually) to indicate one now walks briskly. When the clappers strike one more time one proceeds at the same pace until one reaches one's cushion, bows in gassho and sits again for the next session.

In Japanese *zendos* the cushions will likely be around the edge of the hall, with the altar against a wall, often on the opposite side to the entrance. In a Korean Zen hall, the cushions are usually laid out in two lines more toward the middle of the room. And then in Chinese meditation halls while the cushions are around the edge of the room, the altar will be in the middle of the room.

As to how one mediates, that again varies from tradition to tradition. In Chinese and Japanese Soto Zen, it is quite usual to recommend the beginning student count their breaths. This helps to still the mind, and the goal would be to eventually not need to do the counting. Generally, the guidance is to only count to ten and then start again rather than try to count to a higher number. If one ever loses track of the count, then one simply starts again at one.

Having mastered a natural breathing style with some stilling of the mind through counting, one is then encouraged to move on to just observing the breaths rather than counting them. One breathes normally, and merely observes. Eventually, one can move on to "just sitting" and not need to either still the mind by breath-counting or observing breaths. In the intervening time, at any point one finds one's thoughts taking over—monkey mind we call it—then one reverts to observing breaths again, or even back to counting again. It may help to sit with the thought "*Who is this that is breathing?*" and eventually there will just be breathing.

144

As mentioned earlier in this book, the Caodong tradition (Soto in Japan) espoused the idea of "silent illumination" or "just sitting" (*shikantaza,* Jp; *Mozhao Chan,* Ch). The "Silent" part means simply meditating while having no thoughts. The "illumination" part means simply "clarity." Gradually, in time with this method the mind does not move and is very clear ("pure," as Suzuki put it). The unmoving mind is silent, and the illumined mind is clear.

In the poem written by the Third Ancestor (Jianzhi Sengcan) named "Faith in Mind," he wrote, *"The highest path is not difficult, so long as you are free from discriminations."* He also wrote, *"This principle is neither hurried nor slow. One thought for ten thousand years."* And in his poem "Song of the Silent Illumination," Master Hongzhi Zhengjue, who coined the phrase "silent illumination" (*Mozhao Chan*), wrote:

In silence, words are forgotten.
In utter clarity, things appear.

Yasutani Roshi said in his published interviews:

Shikan-taza is the purest kind of zazen, the practice emphasized by the Soto sect of Zen. Counting the breath and following the breath are expedient devices. A person who can't walk well requires support and all these other methods are such supports. But eventually you must dispense with them and just walk. Shikantaza is zazen in which your mind, intensely involved in just sitting, has nothing to lean on; hence it is a very difficult practice. In counting or following the breath with the mind's eye, you soon know it if you are not doing them properly, but in shikantaza it is easy to become lax, since you have no gauges by which to check yourself.

In the Korean tradition it is more usual to sit with the phrase "What is this?" And in Master Seung Sahn's teaching he adds, "Don't know." This probably derives from the famous exchange that took place between the Sixth Ancestor and his main disciple:

> *Huaijang entered the room and bowed to Huineng.*
> *Huineng asked, "Where do you come from?"*
> *"I came from Mount Sung", replied Huaijang.*
> *"What is this and how did it get here?", demanded Huineng.*
> *Huaijang could not answer and remained speechless.*
> *He practiced for many years until he understood.*
> *He went to see Huineng to tell him about his breakthrough.*
> *Huineng asked, "What is this?"*
> *Huaijang replied, "To say it is like something is not to the point. But still it can be cultivated".*

This short phrase ("What is this?") is what is called a hwadu (*hautou*, Ch) or a head phrase that one is guided to sit with. Hwadu are related to koans (kong-ans) and it may be that in the Zen center one attends there is the opportunity to partake in koan introspection with a teacher.

Koan Introspection

While koan introspection is most associated perhaps with the Japanese Rinzai Zen sect, it is also widely used in Soto Zen sanghas, especially those influenced by the Sanbo Kyodan style devised by Yasutani Roshi and his teacher Harada Daiun Sogaku, which mixed elements of Soto with Rinzai practices. It is also found in Korean Zen practices, which in turn have roots in the Chinese Linji tradition (which became Rinzai in Japan).

Koans (Kong-an, Kr; Gong-an, Ch) like zazen are about waking up. They may appear to be intellectual exercises, seeming to be puzzles or riddles to be solved. But nothing could be further from the truth. Language is used to cut through language to get to before speech, before thinking to an aspect of mind that is truly fundamental. The koans are used to cut through commonplace preconceptions and ways of thinking. But how they are used depends on the tradition.

The Rinzai approach can be very strict and involve an exhaustive koan curriculum. Not only might a student be asked to present to the Roshi on the koan in *sanzen* (interview; *dokusan* in Soto Zen), but may be sent away to discern a poem or capping phrase for the koan in a huge tome named *Zen Sand*. Rinzai teachers have been known to hit their students with a stick if they give an unacceptable presentation on a koan. This is rarer for any Soto school, although its been known at ZCLA, of instance. And it is non-existent in my experience in Korean Zen.

Soto Zen koan introspection is perhaps less intense, but still often highly formalized. Typically, soon after the first session of zazen has started, the Roshi or head teacher will leave the *Zendo* to sit in an interview room nearby. He or she will ring a bell to indicate that the next student wishing *dokusan* is to come to the room. In some centers you simply learn when to join the line, in others there may be a simple system such as a small stick that is passed person to person in the zendo, going clockwise from where the teacher was sitting. If the person wishes a one on one session, then they keep the stick and only pass it to the next person as they get up to go to the interview room

If they do not wish to participate, they simply pass it to the next person in line. When it's one's turn one walks to the interview room, enters respectfully, and one is likely to be required to make at least one full bow on the mat in front of the Roshi. Some teachers may sit in chairs, in which case you do a deep standing bow before sitting down. What is then usual is to simply state to the Roshi, "My name is [dharma name] and my practice is [name of the koan you are working on]." To which the Roshi may simply reply, "And you are here to present on the koan?" Whereupon one is to present.

Because the goal is to use language to cut through language and get before thought, before action, the student may be given just one brief chance to present. For instance, if the Roshi is seeking a non-verbal presentation then the moment the student starts to speak the Roshi may ring her bell indicating the *dokusan* is ended. No protest is permitted, one simply bows and leaves the room. That bell has also called the next student and you must leave promptly.

In this system, there is no discussion of what took place in the interview room unless on the rarer occasion the Roshi invites the student to say why they said or did what they did. Thus, the student may not approach the Roshi outside of the interview room to discuss the koan with him or her, nor usually may the student email or text the Roshi to gain further insight. The attempts at the koan are limited to what may be a matter of a few seconds once a week, if that is the *dokusan* schedule (which it often is). Not all teachers in the Japanese tradition operate this way, but many do.

It is said that there are generally two types of Soto teacher working on koan introspection, the strict master who uses abrupt and even sometimes a little cruel language to try to shock the student into before-thought, and the more "mother hen" style teacher who will be far more gentle with the student. It is not surprising to learn, then, that some students work on the same koan for many months, or even many years.

In the Japanese Zen tradition, its usual to start with the koan *Mu* (*Wu* in Chinese). It is well known to anyone who has studied Buddhism that the Buddha taught that all sentient beings have Buddha-nature. This koan assumes the student knows this teaching, and has a monk asking the famous Chinese Chan Master Zhaozhou Congshen (*Joshu*, Jp):

"Has a dog Buddha-nature or not?"
Zhaozhou answered, "Wu." (Mu)

Wu (or Mu) means "No" or "not have, without." In Chinese culture the dog was about as low down the hierarchy of animals one could get, so in a sense the monk was asking the master, "Although Buddha taught all sentient beings have Buddha-nature, does even the lowly dog have Buddha-nature?" Joshu should have answered "Yes," but instead he said "No."

At first the student may be tempted to give an intellectual answer, but that is not what the teacher is seeking. Rather, the teacher is looking for some evidence the student has attained a basic grasp (or rather realization) of who they are. This koan can often lead to numerous so-called "checking questions" which, as their name implies, help the teacher to check if the student has truly grasped what is sought. This koan is of central importance to some Soto Zen groups in America, and indeed entire books have been written just on this one koan. [1]

The Rinzai Master Hakuin Ekaku (1686-1769) is credited with reviving the Rinzai School in the eighteenth century, and one of the changes he made was to retire the koan Mu as the starting koan and replaced it with a new one he invented. This koan is one that has entered popular culture, and (albeit wrongly stated) is perhaps the most famous koan. The koan is often misstated as *"What is the sound of one hand clapping?"*

That is not what the actual koan states:

"You know the sound of two hands clapping; tell me, what is the sound of one hand?"

Hakuin felt that the Mu koan had become too formalized with the monks having numerous pat answers written down and passed down through generations since the original Chan masters first used it to teach. He thus introduced this fresh new starter-koan, with considerable success.

By contrast, working on koans with a Korean teacher, particularly in the tradition established by Master Seung Sahn, can be a quite different experience. The Chanyuan Qinggui (Zen Buddhist Monastic Code – 1103 C.E.) says that an interview with the teacher can be used to work on koans, but it can also be a time the teacher gets to know the student better, discusses important news of the day, and other topics. Even working on koans can be gentler and more forgiving than in the Soto or Rinzai traditions. Thus, it is not unusual for a Korean Zen teacher to give prompts to the student and help them to appreciate what an acceptable response to a koan might be.

Consequently, an interview session with a Korean Zen teacher can last and hour and take place at prearranged times other than during any formal meditation sitting. Indeed, there is a growing trend for such teacher-pupil interviews to happen using video chat (such as Zoom), both in the Korean and Japanese traditions. This practice understandably grew during the Covid 19 pandemic.

Korean teachers may also start with the koan Mu (or the "Mu cycle" as its come to be known), but they may also start with some more basic grounding-koans, dealing with such questions as "What is truth?" or "When you are born, where do you come from?"

Retreats

If you are a casual follower of the Zen path, you may just have a meditation practice. But if possible, I highly recommend attending a retreat if you are able. Zen retreats in the West usually last two to seven days, and in the Japanese tradition are known as *sesshin*. You will also find one-day retreats, and these are sometimes referred to as *zazenki*. The standard sesshin lasts seven days, and if possible, I recommend when it is possible to attend a week-long retreat since there are distinct benefits from experiencing a week of practice with others.

These Zen retreats are usually silent, which may be a new experience for you. For some, being silent for extended periods is a wonderful experience they crave more of, and for others it is something they find very uncomfortable. If you do find it uncomfortable, then try a one-day silent retreat at first, then look for ones that are 2-3 days, and work up to trying a week-long one.

Some people who meditate on a regular basis and do two sitting sessions at a time often find the second sitting to enable them to go deeper. They feel more relaxed in the second sitting, and report that they spent the first sitting settling in. Well, this experience is expanded on in sesshin—the first few days may present one with challenges, but by the end of the week one may experience a deeper sense of peace and tranquility that many find extremely helpful for their overall practice.

Silent retreats are usually not totally silent the entire time. While most of the time is spent in silence, you may find that the Zen center will designate one meal, for instance, as one attendees may speak at. Although speech is encouraged to be low volume even then. For those not used to silent retreats, there can be some challenging moments, perhaps even some amusing moments. I recall at my first ever retreat at a Zen center in Mendocino, Northern California, during a silent lunch someone started to make hand motions to me. I had no idea what the person was trying to say, and speaking was strictly prohibited. I gave my best "*I don't know what your saying*" face, hand gesture and shoulder shrug, which was followed by even more elaborate hand gestures, his face now very animated.

I still had absolutely no idea what he was trying to say. Was I doing something wrong that he was correcting? Did he want something, and if so what (his gestures while wonderfully varied did not include pointing at anything)? Finally, the Roshi spoke and said in a gentle stage whisper, "*He wants you to pass the salt to him*." I did so, and all those round the table froze as if in a cartoon, forks partly to their wide-open mouths, eyes wide open, all looking at the Roshi unable to process that he had spoken. He ignored them and continued to eat as if nothing had taken place.

In the talks he gave in subsequent days, the Roshi did not mention the event and continued to act as if it had never happened. For days afterwards whenever we were permitted to speak the topic was, *"Can you believe Roshi spoke?! He of all people knows we are not supposed to speak!"* That was back in the days before texting, I can only imagine what the texts would be like if it happened now during a "silent" retreat. This reminds me of the story about an old Zen master and a young monk:

An elderly Zen master was walking with a young monk, and their walk took them along a road that was interrupted by a shallow but fast flowing stream. To continue the route, it was necessary to wade across the stream. As they got to the stream there was a young woman standing on the bank of the stream, clearly trying to work out how she could get across. Now, in this Zen order it was strictly prohibited to talk to a woman, let alone touch one.

In one fluid motion, the old master gently picked the young woman up, carried her across the stream and put her down on the other side.

The master and the novice monk continued their walk in silence. Around a half mile later, the young monk could stand it no longer. "Master!" he said, "We are forbidden to touch a woman, but you carried that young woman across that stream!"

"Young man," replied the old master, "I put the woman down half a mile ago, why are you still carrying her?"

There is a useful teaching here that helps with more than just attendance at a Zen retreat, it can help with our entire practice. When someone else does something they perhaps should not have done, or doesn't do it quite right, or if you do something wrong or less than perfectly, work on *putting it all down*. Don't carry it with you or it will severely impact your practice let alone your ability to be fully present to those around you. Take careful note of what happened, learn from it, store it away to refer back to, should that be appropriate, then let it go. And, of course, if you should apologize, then do so. But then move on.

A Korean Zen retreat in the West is likely to have been adapted from the way it is done in Korea in order to make it more accessible to western practitioners. Rising early, as early as three or four in the morning, is common to Zen retreats, and the day may be started with a period of sitting prior to any breakfast. The sitting sessions tend to be longer than you may be used to, typically forty to fifty minutes each. The breakfast that follows may be informal but may still encourage no speaking or minimal speech.

Unlike other Zen traditions, Korean retreats may not have services or ceremonies, and thus the days may be filled primarily with sitting and walking meditation with a talk by the main teacher toward the end of each day. You may find that the lunch and evening meal are also informal at a Korean retreat, in contrast for instance to the Japanese tradition. There will be a focus on *hwadu*, which may involve spending your days reflecting on the question, "What is this?"

The events over the day are not marked by the sound of bells, but rather by hitting wooden clappers, much as the Japanese tradition may use during the walking meditation sessions. The difference being what is used is a *Jukpi*, a traditional stick that is split about two-thirds of the way down. The teacher holds the stick on one hand and slaps it into the palm of the other hand to mark the start and end of sessions and the start and end of periods of bowing. In Japanese Zen these are called *targykultura* (usually made of bamboo) or *Jookbi* (usually made of wood).

A quick aside: Larger versions of the stick are used in Japanese zazen sessions to give a *kyosaku*, which is a blow given to both shoulders with the stick that is also known as a *keisaku* in Japanese. This stick is also known as the "Stick of Compassion" and in Japanese Zen its used when a student is feeling drowsy or having trouble concentrating. It is only given in the Soto tradition if the student asks for it, but in Rinzai it may be given when a head monk believes it is needed.

In the Korean retreat the only ceremonies are usually a morning and evening period of three formal bows. Usually, attendance at these sessions is optional.

Chinese Chan retreats can be far more demanding. They are designed to be a challenge to the student and may be partly intended to frustrate the attendee. One rises very early and the days last until fairly late, perhaps ten o'clock or later. Having risen at three or four a.m., these days can feel very long. During the day there is a mixture of meditation, walking, and working—the work can include almost anything that might need to be done from helping in the kitchen to working in the yard, repairing fences, or planting vegetables.

Talks will be given by teachers during the day, and there will be periods of liturgy and chanting. All meals are very formal, and always in silence. Indeed, one of the key challenges for some attendees is that the entire week is essentially in silence.

Japanese retreats lean toward the greater formality of a Chan retreat, but with silence not being observed at absolutely all times and some meals being less formal. As is often the case with Japanese Zen practice, whether Soto or Rinzai, one is required to wear black clothing, or at least dark clothing with no images or words on t-shirts if they are worn.

Be prepared to be faced with a long list of rules when attending a Japanese Zen retreat: this is where the recommendation to "put it all down" can come in handy, don't dwell on any thoughts that may arise about the formality or restrictions. Let it be part of your practice to pass through them to freedom from them. The rules will govern precisely when events will happen, what you may or may not do during each part of the day, admonition not to speak generally, with certain times when quiet speaking is permitted.

Bells will be used to mark the start of new sessions, but often the *han* (large wooden block hit with a wooden mallet) will be hit to summon you to the next event. Sitting sessions in the *zendo* will be very formal, with even the slightest sound discouraged. Although possibly not required, you will find some attendees will continue sitting zazen through the night on some occasions. Here is a fairly detailed schedule from a *sesshin* at Upaya Zen Center in New Mexico:

First Day:

5:30 - 6:30 p.m. Oryoki Instruction

6:30 Dinner

7:45 - 9:00 Sesshin Orientation

9:00 Four Vows

9:20 - 10:00 Optional Sit

Full Days:

5:00 - 5:40 a.m. Optional Sit

5:30 Wake up Bell

6:00 - 7:40 Meditation Instruction (1st full day only)
  Kentan/Zazen/Kinhin

7:40 Service

8:00 Breakfast

9:30 Samu

10:30 Rest

11:00 Zazen/Dharma Talk (except Wednesday)

12:00 p.m. Zazen

12:40 Service

1:00 Lunch

3:00 - 4:00 Zazen/Kinhin

4:00 - 5:00 Dharma Walk/Qigong

5:00 Rest

5:30 Zazen/Kinhin (Dharma Talk Wednesday night
  only)

6:30 Dinner

7:45 - 8:45 Zazen/Kinhin

8:45 Vows

9:00 - 10:00 Optional Sit

Last Day:
6:00 - 6:40 a.m. Optional Sit
6:30 Wake up Bell
7:00 - 7:40 Kentan/Zazen
7:40 Service
8:00 Breakfast
9:15 Closing Council
11:00 Samu
12:30 p.m. Lunch

"Samu" is work and can be almost anything that needs doing on the campus. Usually, there will be lists posted that assign attendees to certain tasks such as kitchen duty, temple cleaning duty, gardening, and so on. One might be assigned the same samu task for the whole week, or it may change day to day. "Kentan" are checking rounds done by senior teachers while sitting zazen. "Qijong" is a very old Chinese system of postures and breathing practice. You are not likely to have such a session at other Zen centers, but Upaya has introduced it as a staple of its retreats over the years. Last, a "Dharma Walk" is usually a meditative walk in the nearby woods.

Although not mentioned in this sample schedule, Zen *sesshins* often include a period of time where one can meet for an interview with the Roshi or a senior retreat teacher (one-on-one session; *dokusan*, Jp). I've described elsewhere in this book how these formal interviews happen, and once again like the rest of the retreat they are guided by specific rules that must be followed.

When attending a Zen retreat you will be exposed to who you are in a way that you are not used to doing. For instance, you will soon find out how you cope with extended periods of silence, of sitting even when it is uncomfortable to do so, and how you deal with your thoughts that won't stop or the emotions that arise for you. At the best retreats there will be someone leading the retreat, or one of the teachers, who you can book time with to discuss any issues you are facing. But in some Zen centers you are entirely on your own and with a prohibition on speaking, you may not even be able to chat with a fellow attendee about your issues.

Some Zen teachers want you to feel a degree of discomfort and frustration since they believe you will grow in your practice from it. For instance, at Upaya for many years (it may still be true) all beds in the residences are relatively hard futons. For those who have significant back issues, there may be a regular mattress available, but for the rest one may be facing sleepless nights and hence all the more exhausting days. But know that taking yourself to a limit in this way can be very freeing, and that is undoubtedly part of the intent.

Sleepless nights, of course, can cause you to feel very drowsy during zazen, so it can be a challenge to stay awake during sessions. Everyone has their own way to address this—not for nothing Zen recommends open-eyed meditation, and sitting up straight, both of which make one less likely to be sleepy. Some attendees have their own methods of dealing with sleepiness, such as holding the bridge of their nose briefly—some swear this works, others say it does nothing for them. But you can take the opportunity of the strike of the split-stick on the shoulders when it is offered, if that helps. You'll notice the mention of "oryoki training" in this sample schedule. Oryoki is a very formal way of eating a meal that involves a set of bowls, chop sticks, a wooden spatula, a wooden spoon and a cloth. The oryoki session is highly formal—it takes place in silence and one has the courses of the meal brought to you by those assigned to the task of acting in a waiter style role. The oryoki set is initially wrapped up in the cloth in a very specific way and has to be unwrapped.

Each of the bowls is for a specific purpose, and a basic premise of everything being eaten to the last speck, and the bowls cleaned with a liquid served toward the end of the meal (often a weak mint tea), cleaned with the cloth after you drink the tea mixed with whatever was left in your bowls.

If you have food allergies, then it will be important to let the retreat leader (or cook) know before the oryoki session since the rule is that you cannot leave anything in a bowl. There is also nowhere to dispose of anything where you sit for the meal. I recall one instance where a person sitting next to me asked the person in the waiter role if the meal contained potato since he is allergic. The assistant said there was not. But when the meal was being dished out into our bowls, I spotted immediately that there was potato in it.

I met the gaze of the person next to me, and although not permitted, I held out my main food bowl to him so that he could unload his portion of potatoes into my bowl. He smiled and gave a slight bow, his face that had moments ago shown abject horror now revealed a deep sense of relief. Again, carrying the woman across the stream—sometimes you are called on to do something and you will know in the moment what that is. Do it. Then move on.

One last vignette about carrying something around on retreat only to then discover what you were carrying was what you brought with you to the retreat—your misconceptions and preconceptions. At one week-long sesshin there was always one woman who was late to zazen. We attendees were warned over and again to arrive at least ten minutes early and get to our seats. Some still persisted in arriving barely a few minutes before we started, but this one woman always walked in after the Roshi was already seated.

Roshi had set aside some time where attendees could break the general great silence and in hushed terms, raise issues they had with the retreat. One attendee could bear it no longer, *"That woman keeps being late to zazen! It's so rude that we are all asked to be there early, and she always turns up late!"* The Roshi gave the person a compassionate nod, and said, *"That woman, as you call her, is my head monk whose job it is to strike the han to call you all to the zendo. It is her job to keep hitting the han until all have entered, including me. Then, and only then, does she stop hitting the han and enter the zendo herself."*

Do I need a Teacher?

A few final words on this topic. If you are going to be a casual follower of the Zen way, you may only be practicing zazen on, hopefully, some kind of regular basis. Certainly, if you want to go deeper, do koan introspection, or even perhaps explore the track to become a monk, nun, priest or teacher, then a teacher will be essential. But I would say even if you are just casually sitting from time to time, a teacher or mentor can still be extremely useful. I have lost count of the number of people who have told me they have been sitting zazen for decades and still their mind is racing all the time, or still they are in extreme pain if they try to sit for more than ten minutes.

Having a teacher or mentor who you can talk to, even if its is just about your zazen practice, can be invaluable. Indeed, recalling the Three Treasures, Zen is about being in community and having this interaction with others. We walk this path together, if you think you are walking it alone then that is a delusion.

---

[1] James Ishmael Ford, Melissa Lyozen Blacker (Eds), *The Book of Mu: Essential Writings on Zen's Most Important Koan*, Wisdom Publications, 2011.

further reading

Being Upright: Zen Meditation and the Bodhisattva Precepts, Reb Anderson, Rodmell Press, 2000

The Blue Cliff Record, Thomas Cleary, Shambala 2005

The Book of Equanimity: Illuminating Classic Zen Koans, Gerry Shishin Wick

Christ Way, Buddha Way: Jesus as Wisdom Teacher and a Zen Perspective on His Teachings, Tim Langdell, StillCenter Publications, 2020

The Compass of Zen Seung Sahn, Shambala 1997

Crooked Cucumber: The Life and Zen Teaching of Shunryu Suzuki, David Chadwick, Harmony, 2000

Don't Be A Jerk: And Other Practical Advice from Dogen, Japan's Greatest Zen Master, Brad Warner New World Library 2016

Dropping Ashes on the Buddha: The Teachings of Zen Master Seung Sahn, Grove Press, 1994

Everyday Zen: Love and Work, by Charlotte Joko Beck, HarperOne, 2007

The Gateless Gate: The Classic Book of Zen Koans,– Koun Yamada Wisdom Publications, 2004

Hardcore Zen, Brad Warner Wisdom Publications 2003

Instructions to the Cook: A Zen Master's Lessons in Living a Life That Matters – Bernard Glassman, Harmony Books 1996

An Introduction to Zen Buddhism, DT Suzuki Grove Press, 1994

Introduction to Zen Koans: Learning the Language of Dragons, James Ishmael Ford, Wisdom Publications 2018

The Mind of Clover: Essays in Zen Buddhist Ethics, Robert Aitken, North Point Press 2015

The Book of Mu: Essential Writings on Zen's Most Important Koan, James Ishmael Ford, Melissa Lyozen Blacker (Eds), Wisdom Publications, 2011

On Having No Head, Douglas Harding, The Sholland Trust, 2013

Only Don't Know: Selected Teaching Letters of Zen Master Seung Sahn, Seung Sahn Shambala, 1999

Opening the Hand of Thought, Kosho Uchiyama, Wisdom Publications, 2004

The Rinzai Zen Way: A Guide to Practice, Meido Moore, Shambala, 2018

Sitting with Koans: Essential Writings on Zen Koan Introspection, John Daido Loori (ed), Wisdom Publications, 2009

Taking the Path of Zen, Robert Aitken, North Point Press, 1982

Ten Gates: The Kong-an Teaching of Zen Master Seung Sahn, Shambala, 2007

Thorsens Principles of Zen, Martine Batchelor, Thorsens, 1999 (Out of print, you may find a used copy)

The Three Pillars of Zen: Teaching, Practice, and Enlightenment, Roshi Philip Kapleau, Alfred. K. Knopf, 1989

Treasury of the True Dharma Eye: Zen Master Dogen's Shobo Genzo, Kazuaki Tanahashi, Shambala, 2013

Treasury of the Eye of True Teaching: Chan Master Dahui's Classic Work (Vols I & II), Thomas Cleary, Kindle only, 2017

The Way of Korean Zen – Kusan Sunim, Weatherhill, 2009

The Way of Zen of Zen, Alan Watts, Vintage, 1999

The Zen Teaching of Bodhidharma, Red Pine (Trans.) North Point Press, 1989

Zen Flesh Zen Bones: A Collection of Zen and Pre-Zen Writings, Paul Reps, Tuttle Publishing, 1998

Zen's Chinese Heritage, Andy Ferguson, Wisdom Publications, 2011

Zen Sand, Victor Sogen Hori, University of Hawaii Press, 2010

Zen Mind, Beginner's Mind: Informal Talks on Zen Meditation and Practice, Shunryu Suzuki, Shambala, 2011

Zen: A Way of Life, Christmas Humphreys, English Universities Press, 1962 (Out of print, you may find a used copy)

Zen Keys: A Guide to Zen Practice, Thich Nhat Hanh, Harmony, 1994

glossary of terms

Bodhisattva—one who lives for the benefit of all beings. It can be used to refer to a historic person or to one's essential nature, being "How may I help you?"

Buddha Hall— name given to the room or building reserved for services and ceremonies" in some cases (where there is no separate Dharma Hall) for lectures.

Ch'an (or Chan)— the original "Zen" the Buddhist sect that was founded in China in around the 6th century, legend saying the teachings were brought there by Bodhidharma.

Chiden— the person who takes care of the altars. This task requires trimming the candle, cleaning out incense bowls, and brushing the dust from the statues and altar cloths.

Densho— a large bell which is rung to announce a service or a talk.

Dharma—variously defined and used as the way the universe works (the law of the universe), the teachings of the Buddha or Buddhism, and elements or forms of the world.

Doan-ryo—the group of people who serve in temple roles—the doan, jisha, kokyo, fukudo, and doshi.

Doan—person who rings the bells for service and for meditation. They also have several other tasks in the temple.

Dokusan—a formal one on one meeting with a teacher, also referred to as an interview.

Doshi—the ordained priest who leads the service.

Eightfold Path: The Eightfold path was given by the Buddha as part of the Four Noble Truths and as such, as the main way out of suffering.

1. Right View (Understanding)
2. Right Intention
3. Right Speech
4. Right Conduct
5. Right Livelihood
6. Right Effort
7. Right Mindfulness
8. Right Meditation

Engawa— Wooden walkway surrounding a zendo.

Fukudo—the person who drums on the mokugyo.

Four Noble Truths: The Four Noble Truths are the answer that came to the Buddha as part of his awakening.

1. Suffering is all around us; it is a part of life
2. The cause of suffering is craving and attachment
3. There is a way out; craving can be ended and thus suffering can be ended
4. The way to end craving is the Eightfold Path

Gassho—a hand gesture of holding palms together (similar to the way hands are held in Christian prayer). Gassho is held with the elbows out, the hands held a few inches from the lower part of the face.

Han— Wooden block suspended on rope and struck with a mallet to summon monks to the zendo or to a practice hall.

Ino— person who is in charge of the zendo (mediation hall).

Inkin— Small portable bell sitting on top of a lacquered stick with a small decorative cushion in between. The bell is struck with a long pin-like striker.

Ji Do Poep Sa Nim (JDPSN)— Dharma master (also known as a Master Zen Teacher) in the Korean Seong (Zen) tradition.

Jikido— Person with a variety of duties in a Zen center such as lighting and extinguishing lamps, striking a secondary han, striking a work drum or bell for samu (work practice).

Jiki-Jitsu (Jiko)— A timekeeper for meditation sessions.

Jisha— person who carries the incense for offering. During retreats, the jisha may be in charge of sign-ups for practice discussion or dokusan.

Jukai—the Soto Zen ceremony for receiving the precepts.

Karma— Buddhist doctrine of cause and effect.

Kensho— Literally means to "see nature" and is a term used when someone has a glimpse into their true nature.

Kinhin— walking meditation.

Koan—a Zen story known as a "public case" that is designed to help a student realize their true self. Koan introspection is done with a teacher.

Kokyo—the person who calls out the chants during service.

Mahayana— The "Great Vehicle," the branch of Buddhism that started around 2,000 years ago and more emphasis is placed on saving all beings rather than achieving personal salvation.

Mokugyo— wooden drum used for some chants.\

Mudra—a hand gesture such as gassho or shashu.

Nirvana— literally means "blowing out" or "quenching" it is the highest goal in Theravada Buddhism. However, in Mahayana Buddhism, of which Zen is part, the student gives up the goal to attain nirvana for himself and instead focuses on saving all sentient beings.

Okesa (Kesa)—the large patched (over) robe worn by priests over the left shoulder, and under the right shoulder.

Oryoki— formal silent meal practice.

Practice Discussion— and informal interview with a Zen teacher or Practice Leader.

Practice Leader— Someone in certain Zen centers or traditions assigned to help students with their practice.

Rakusu— a small replica of the Buddha's robes that is in the form of a bib worn around the neck. Typically, one receives a rakusu after completing the precepts (jukai) in the Soto tradition, and the teacher will often write something on the rear.

Rohatsu— date commemorating the Buddha's awakening, traditionally celebrated on 8 December. It is often the last day of a Rohatsu sesshin, a seven-day intensive retreat.

Roshi— this is a title used to refer to older, revered teachers. In its original use it is reserved for teachers who are over 60 years of age, but in the West it has come to be associated with people who have received full dharma transmission (*inka shomei*)

Ryo— Japanese for a "chamber" or "section," hence "doan ryo" is the instrument player section and "tenzo ryo" is the head cook section.

Samsara— The Buddhist idea of the cycle of birth and death.

Samu—manual labor done with mindfulness.

Sangha— a Zen community or can be used to refer to the larger Zen community of all colleagues (sometimes called the MahaSangha).

Satori— deep insight into one's true self; similar to *kensho* and while there is disagreement over use of the terms, satori is often used for a more complete awakening to one's true nature.

Seiza— A meditation position where the sitter is kneeling, sitting back on their heels.

Sensei— a recognized teacher of Zen in the Japanese tradition.

Sesshin—a silent, intensive Zen retreat. Meals are usually eaten oryoki style and the teacher usually offers participants dokusan.

Shashu— the mudra used for generally walking around a Zen center or its campus grounds. The right hand is wrapped around the top of the fist with the thumb resting on the top of the first hand.

Shika—The person who takes care of guests of the temple.

Shikantaza— Literally "nothing but sitting" and is a core principle in Zen Master Dogen's teachings about doing only zazen whole-heartedly or single-mindedly.

Shoten—the person who sounds the densho to announce events in the Buddha Hall.

Shuso—head student in a practice period.

Soen Sa Nim (Zen master)— honorific or title for a Master Zen Teacher in the Korean Zen tradition who has received full dharma transmission from his or her teacher. In general use in the West, this is equivalent to the title Roshi in Japanese Zen.

Soji— a brief period of mindful work, usually centered on temple cleaning, including caring for the temple grounds.

Sutra— Buddhist scriptures.

Tan—the raised platform on which practitioners sit in meditation in a zendo.

Tanto— person in charge of practice in the temple.

Tatami— the Japanese thick straw mats found in many Zen temples, especially in the zendo.

Tenken— person who sounds the han or densho to call people to zazen or a service, and who plays the mokugyo during a service.

Tenzo— the cook. The tenzo is a central role in the leadership of a sesshin (retreat). The practice of cooking is a vital practice, much like meditation.

Zabuton— the thick square or rectangular mat on which practitioners sit in meditation. The zafu (cushion) is placed on the zabuton.

Zafu— round cushion practitioners sit in meditation.

Zazen— meditation.

Zazenkai— literally means to come together and is the name usually given to a retreat of shorter duration than a sesshin.

Zendo—the meditation hall.

appendix

Who was Bodhidharma?

I think we can go one step better than I did in the earlier chapter to trace who Bodhidharma was and where he came from, if indeed he was a real historical person. The Yue-Chi (also known as the Yuezhi) were an ancient nomadic tribe that hailed from western China. A common theory is that they were an Indo-European people who thus did not look like the Chinese people. During the period from around 170 B.C.E. to around 30 C.E. they migrated west, first clashing with the Wusun people further to the west, and then working their way down to Bactria and then to the Indian Subcontinent.

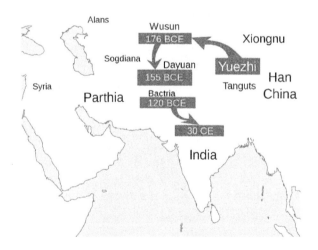

A main faction of the Yue-Chi split off, a tribe known as the Kushans and it is they who created the Kushan empire. This is the empire that replaced the Greco-Buddhist empire established during the period prior to the common era. The Kushan's adopted Buddhism as their national religion, and commenced to spread Buddhism back to the east, to China. By this time the Silk Road was well established, and the Greco-Buddhist empire had already spread Buddhism east to Palestine and the heart of the Hellenist world in Alexandria, Egypt:

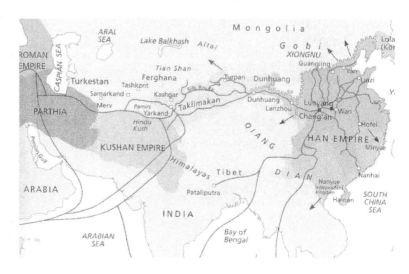

The Silk Road, then, ran back west through the area of the Wusun, and on to the center of the Han Empire as it was in around 200 C.E. By the 4th and 5th centuries when Bodhidharma is said to have come to China the country had formed into two main territories: The Northern and the Southern dynasties (386 C.E. to 589 C.E.). At this time, any Wusun who had become integrated into the Buddhist culture that had its roots in the Greco-Buddhist empire and the Kush, would have naturally been able to travel east to these two Chinese dynasties. Indeed, the Kushan empire is documented to have spread Buddhism into China. Hence, the Yue-Chi, having started in China, moved west to create the Kushan empire, and then spread Buddhism back east along the Silk Road, to where they hailed from and then further east to the main Chinese territories. Bodhidharma was one of these Buddhist emissaries who most likely was of Wusun decent.

about the author

Born in Oxford, England, Tim Langdell is both a Zen Priest and Master Zen Teacher in the Korean and Vietnamese traditions and has over 40 years of practice in the Soto Zen tradition. Tim is also an ordained Christian Priest in the Independent Catholic Church (in communion with the Episcopal Church) and member of a Thomasine Order. He became passionate about Zen and Mystical Christianity at age 19, when he had what he would now describe as a mystical experience, or *kensho*. He became a life-professed member of the Anglican *Third Order of St. Francis* around that time, too.

Tim has lived in Pasadena, California since around 1990, while spending time in his beloved Oxford whenever he can. Tim gained his MDiv at Claremont School of Theology where he also studied at Bloy House Episcopal Seminary. He also holds a PhD in clinical psychology from University College, London, an MA in Educational and Clinical Child Psychology from Nottingham University, and a BS (known in the UK as a BSc) in Physics and Psychology from Leicester University.

Tim is the Abbot and Guiding Teacher at the Pasadena Zen Center (known as StillCenter), and he is Rector of The Church of the Beloved Disciple, too. He is ordained and trained as a Zen teacher in the *Five Mountain Zen Order*, where his ordinations are in the Korean and Vietnamese Zen traditions. His teacher in FMZO is the Venerable Wonji Dharma (Paul Lynch). Tim has over 40 years of practice in the Japanese Soto Zen tradition, mainly through association with the Zen Center of Los Angeles where he trained under Taizan Maezumi, Bernie Glassman and Egyoku Nakao. Tim received Japanese Soto Zen Priest training from Sensei Gyokei Yokoyama. He was also trained as a Buddhist Chaplain at Upaya Zen Center, under Roshi Joan Halifax, with training by Bernie Glassman, Alan Senauke, Kaz Tanahashi, Frank Ostaseski, and others. Tim is a Board-Certified Chaplain, having gained certification with the Association for Professional Chaplains. He is ordained in the independent Catholic movement, originally through the American Catholic Church (established 1915), and his lineage there includes ordination with the Philippine Independent Church which is in full communion with the Episcopal Church. He is a fully ordained Priest in the Ecumenical Catholic Church which is the only independent Catholic group to be a member of the National Council of Churches.

Tim is by training and by passion, a chaplain, a psychologist, an astrophysicist, a computer scientist, an author, and a musician (blues guitar and Middle Eastern oud). He currently serves as the staff chaplain at a hospice in the Los Angeles area of Southern California. He is an author of books on various topics from how to design and code computer games, to dealing with Alzheimer's, to coping with vision loss, as well as books on Zen, Christian meditation and other spiritual topics. He has also written a fantasy novel in the style of Douglas Adams and intends to write more fiction.

He is married to his wife Cheri, an English Professor, has two children, several grandchildren, two cats and a parrot. He and his wife live in Pasadena, California.

www.timlangdell.com, www.stillcenter.org
www.christbuddha.org, www.christwaybuddhaway.com
and Tim's non-profit, www.kids-rights.org

Printed in Great Britain
by Amazon

66848411R00108